I don't usually write revie\~ moment I picked this up, ~~.. .. .. of a young man in a tough city. The mental images produced by the printed version of the life and thoughts of Gabriel Nieves lead me to experience his pain, his joy, and his salvation. Through these pages I witnessed the terrible combination of nature and nurture in one human being . . . a perfect storm. Then I witnessed the transformation that can only by produced by a God who is willing and able to climb into the depths of the sewers for His children. If you, or anyone you know, is struggling with the idea that they have exceeded God's grace, do yourself a favor and pick up this book.

Alex Marroquin
International evangelist

A deep story about making it through the darkest times of life and finding your light and life in Christ. I promise you will be deeply moved.

Andy Vargas
Lead singer, Santana
Founder of Souleros

I know and love Gabriel's story. This is an amazing Jesus story! God is doing great things in and through this man's life.

Pastor Brian Broderson
Calvary Chapel Costa Mesa

The events in this book are true and a real part of many youngsters' lives today. I believe that lives will be touched by Gabriel's story! May God get the glory, honor, and praise for all the good things He has done in and through Gabriel's life.

Ernest " Kilroy " Roybal
Ex-founder of The Mexican Mafia
Founder of Homiez 4 Christ Ministries

When God does a work in a man; nothing can stop Him! Gabriel's story is evidence of that statement being true. Here you have a man that was as far away from God as he could possibly be, even to the point of having no regard for life itself, but JESUS! Once a hurting man of reckless atrocities and looking at life in prison, but now a man without fear, on a mission to share Jesus with as many people as possible. This book will inspire all who read it, it will help people to know the power of God, and it will show that God saves all who turn to Him. God bless!

Pastor Gerry Brown
Founder of U-Turn For Christ

This book gripped, inspired, and challenged me. I believe it literally will change thousands of lives with the grace and love of Jesus Christ. It will inspire and remind many believers that they can make a lasting difference in pursuing God's purposes for their lives.

Pastor Roy Valverde
Victory Outreach International

Gabriel's life is an amazing example of how God kept showing up at just the right time and place. This book will encourage you to never see anyone as hopeless. Looking at Gabriel's childhood, he was definitely on the wrong path. But his story is a testimony to those in the law enforcement community that gang members do change. As you read about Gabriel's life, you will understand the gang culture better and the pressures some young people experience as they grow up. I remember when Gabriel was in juvenile hall, and little did I know we would be ministering together years later.

Chaplain Rick Johnson
Pacific Youth Correctional Ministries
Orange County Probation Facilities

This is a great story of how God can take a life that has gone through many challenges and bring restoration. Through Gabriel's life we see God take brokenness and turn it into something beautiful. This book will bless you.

Pastor Tommy Cota
Hope Alive Church

BEYOND THE GANG

THE REAL-LIFE STORY OF CHRISTIAN RAPPER GABRIEL NIEVES

GABRIEL NIEVES & MIKE LUTZ

*Beyond the Gang: The Real-Life Story
of Christian Rapper Gabriel Nieves*
by Gabriel Nieves and Mike Lutz

Printed in the United States of America.

International Standard Book Number: 9781092398336

24 23 22 21 20 19   7 6 5 4 3 2 1

TABLE OF CONTENTS

FOREWORD

My name is Jeff Blair, and I am the deputy chief of the Tustin Police Department. I have been a Tustin Police Officer for thirty years. Early in my career, I was selected to be a founding member of the Tustin Gang Unit. With a rise in gang-related crimes such as murder, robbery, assault, and theft, the Tustin Police Department formed a five-man gang unit, and we were considered the "tip of the spear" in the war on gangs back then.

We used to cruise the streets of Tustin in an undercover Cadillac Coupe de Ville that was confiscated during a large-scale narcotics operation. The majority of our patrolling was focused on the southwest area of the city, which bordered the much busier city of Santa Ana. Once you headed westbound on McFadden Avenue and crossed over the 55-freeway overpass, you entered a geographic area we referred to as RD13. This was simply police code for Reporting District 13 and allowed us to easily track and report crime activity by region. It was a small geographic region, but due to the high-density apartment complexes, it was heavily populated and made it a hotbed of gang activity. There were only a handful of streets in RD13, and directly in the middle of RD13 was a long two-lane residential street lined with multiplex apartments. This was the headquarters to one of Tustin's most notorious gangs.

This gang claimed all of RD13 as their "turf," but anytime we were out looking for members of the gang to be loitering, we headed over to this small two-lane road in the heart of gangland. Whenever we pulled up, it was not uncommon to find a dozen or more twelve- to fourteen-year-old Hispanic kids hanging out in the south alley adjacent to the carports. The moment our Coupe de Ville would turn the corner, you could count on four or five shaved heads scattering in different directions while a few others stayed put in order to keep us focused on them, rather than those who fled on foot. We were not stupid; we knew the runners were the ones holding the drugs and guns, but they were smart, too. It was a crapshoot if we focused on the right runners, because they would use some of the other runners as decoys.

It was in this alley that I first met Gabriel Nieves, who was better known as Grim. Grim was short for Grim Reaper. Grim was one of the youngsters in the gang, and at that time he was definitely a foot soldier and not a shot caller yet. Even though he was only fifteen years old when I first met him, he was definitely the biggest kid in the gang. Grim was quiet, never disrespectful, but difficult to build a rapport with. He was always guarded in his answers and gave as little information as possible when questioned. Based on his age, size, and demeanor we knew he was the one most likely "putting in work" for the gang, in other words, doing the gang's dirty work. There was no doubt in our minds that he was a main foot soldier packing the guns, dope, and carrying out whatever wicked assignments the gang sent him on.

Because this was an up-and-coming gang, they were collecting enemies at a record pace, and it seemed like we were responding to reports of gunshots on this small two-lane street on a nightly basis. Usually by the time we arrived, there was nobody around and no signs of a shooting, except for this one night when we responded once again to a call of shots being fired in that area of RD13 we were so familiar with. Upon our arrival, Grim and a few of the more active members of the gang were sitting on the curb. Of course, they denied being involved in any sort of shooting and even suggested that the reported noises came from a car backfiring. We actually believed them until an anonymous caller reported that he had captured the shooting on video. This was before the days of digital video and camera phones, so I snuck away from the group to meet the caller at his apartment nearby. He turned on his VCR and showed me the footage he captured from his balcony. It was clear that Grim and his fellow gang members were victims of a drive-by shooting. They were off the hook this time, but it wouldn't be long before Grim would get caught.

One night while out "patrolling," one of the gangs younger members stumbled across a party that was being attended by gang members from Garden Grove. Since their presence in another gang's territory was a sign of disrespect, this youngster rallied up the troops and they decided to confront the partygoers out in front of the complex. Grim was one of those summoned to assist, and like a good soldier, he was right there on the front line. One thing led to another, and before long shots were flying in both directions. It didn't take us long, and we were able to put together a case against Grim and a few other shooters.

After I was promoted to the rank of sergeant, I was transferred out of the gang unit right after these arrests. I knew Grim had been charged with attempted murder along with some other gang-related charges, but after being transferred out of the gang unit I lost track of most of these guys. I did eventually learn that Grim beat the rap due to some inconsistent witness statements.

It has been almost twenty years since those arrests, and through the years, and the promotions, my favorite assignment was being a member of Tustin's first Gang Unit when the sound of gunfire crackling in the distance was common.

A few months ago, I received a message from the man formerly known as Grim. He wrote me to tell me that he had found God and was doing gang intervention and outreach work. These words were written for José Gabriel Nieves, man of God, not for Grim the street soldier.

Deputy Chief Jeff Blair
Tustin Police Department
Tustin, California

BEYOND THE GANG

CHAPTER 1

SEX, DRUGS, AND GANG PATROL

He heals the brokenhearted
And binds up their wounds.
(Psalm 147:3)

I was awakened by screams and sobbing coming from my mother's bedroom. At five years old, I was already accustomed to hearing my mom being beaten by my stepdad. On this particular night I wanted to drown out the hysterical cries for help, so I did the only thing a five-year-old could think to do, which was to hide under the covers and bury my head beneath my pillow. I wish I could say this was a rare, once-in-a lifetime experience, but unfortunately, it was a way of life.

I grew up in a home where abuse was not the exception but the rule. The strange irony is that I loved this man I called Dad because, like most kids, I was desperate to have the love of a father in my life. But as much as I wanted this relationship, especially because I had no way of knowing my biological father, it was not meant to be.

By the age of six, my mom and stepdad had another child, and I soon realized that I would become more and more invisible to Dad as he focused his love and affection on his own flesh-and-blood son.

I took some minor comfort in knowing that my mom loved me. But that love fell short, because in my day-to-day life she was never home. Working two and three jobs to help pay the bills also meant that what little time was spent at home was filled up with the drudgery of life's daily essentials. The result was that I not only felt unloved, but I was also left to care for myself much of the time.

Starting with Kindergarten, I would wake myself up for school, get myself dressed, get my own breakfast, and walk myself to school. Living like this forced me to grow up faster than I wanted and faster than any kid should.

Growing up with an abusive stepfather, an overworked mother, and never knowing my real dad made me an angry kid. I never saw the bright side of life. I lived on the dark side of hopelessness. Add to that the regular beatdowns I took from many bigger kids on the block, which only fueled the fire of my anger. My life was a pressure cooker. It was not so much of *if* I would explode, but more of *when*. Eventually my anger would find a way out.

Every kid needs stability, but the only constant in my life was the awareness that we would move every few years. The financial hardships we faced were complicated by the fact that my stepdad was a violent, functional alcoholic. Although he was able to hold down a job during the day, when he was off the clock he would drink and get drunk. It was his way of escaping his responsibilities. But those responsibilities always came knocking, and when they did, it was usually in the form of an eviction notice.

Dad had his escape, and by the sixth grade I found an escape of my own. It was an escape that didn't involve alcohol, drugs, or violence, at least not at this point in my life. My escape was basketball. I remember trying out for the Boys Club basketball team and discovered that I actually had some natural talent when it came to playing hoops. The feeling I had while on the court, the excitement of being part of a team, and realizing that I was actually good at something was the best feeling I had experienced so far in my life. I loved basketball so much that it was the first time I allowed myself to dream for something bigger and better for my life. I wanted to be an all-star player in the NBA. And because I stood six-foot-three by the seventh grade, I felt like I actually had a chance at realizing that dream. There were very few Mexican players who had ever made it to the NBA, and I wanted to be one of the few who made it.

During this time of playing basketball, I became friends with a kid named Kobie. My close friendship with him was a bright spot in my youth. I would often spend time at his house because we got along so well and it got me out of my house, where things were always unpredictable and often unhealthy.

One Saturday night I was over at Kobie's house, where we were watching NBA videos as we often did. The time got away from us, and before we knew it, it was very late. When he asked if I wanted to stay over, I of course I jumped at the offer, because the last place I wanted to be was at home. I knew my dad would be drunk by that time, which meant nothing good was waiting for me at home.

"Okay," Kobie said. "Let me just ask my mom." When he came back, he told me that his mom said I could spend the night, but I would have to go to church with them in the morning. "Hey, I understand if you don't want to do the church thing," he said. "It's cool."

My response was quick and immediate. "Hey man, let's go to church, then!"

Little did I know that it would be the beginning of something new for me. I had never been to a Christian church before in my life. God and all that religion stuff just wasn't something I was ever exposed to. If you would have asked me prior to my going to church that Sunday, I would have said something like, "I know a few guys named Jesús, but God? I ain't never seen God in the 'hood."

I remember walking into church that Sunday and feeling a little out of place and a little uncomfortable at first. But a few minutes into the service, I let down my guard and began to simply listen to the sermon. I don't remember what the pastor spoke about that day, but what I do remember is that I felt at home there. At twelve years old, I had seen a lot, been through a lot, and experienced a lot of hardships, but I had not experienced a lot of love. There at church I felt loved and accepted. It had such an impact on me that I couldn't wait to go back the next week and the week after that. After a few weeks, I found out that the church had a youth group, which I also started attending weekly. Over the next few months, I was really thriving at that church, and it all led me to give my life to Jesus.

Even though I found a peace and a love in Christ that I had never experienced before, the chaos continued at home. And yet again due to financial trouble at home, the knock on the door came once again. We had been evicted and were forced to move. This time we moved in with my aunt. And unlike the previous moves, this one would prove to be devastating for me.

Things had been going so well. I was excelling at basketball, my friendships were great, and I was enjoying my new decision to follow Jesus. But as good as life was going, evil was right there to ruin my plans.

There is a verse in the Bible that says, "Bad company corrupts good character" (1 Corinthians 15:33 NIV), and I can bear witness to that fact. In this next stage of my life, I was surrounded by bad company, which undeniably corrupted my personality, my behavior, and my attitude.

I had a couple of older cousins who often came by my aunt's house, and these guys were always bragging about how they came from "the neighborhood." This just meant they were in the gang. At first I couldn't help but think how these guys were so dumb. All their talk about "the neighborhood" seemed like a waste of time, and it was nothing I wanted for myself. I was focused on going to the NBA, and all the stuff they were into seemed, well, just stupid. So I kept working on my basketball dream, but that, too, was now becoming more and more difficult for me.

I was out there doing everything on my own. I had to get myself to practice and games, and with the financial troubles my family had, I had to ask for help to cover my expenses to play. I tried getting scholarships and financial aid just so I could keep playing. Despite all these challenges, I was still encouraged. While I was in the eighth grade. our school team was good. We were winning and excelling in our division. For me this meant my dream of the NBA was still alive. But that was all about to change. One bad decision, one momentary lapse in judgment, one moment of uncontrolled anger would forever change the direction of my life and turn my dreams into nothing more than wishful thinking.

It happened one day when a kid picked a fight with me. I am not sure why, but I am sure it was something I could have just walked away from. Sadly, I did not make that choice that day. Something deep inside of me snapped when he made his move against me, and all the rage I had been pushing down day after day, year after year, no longer could be ignored. I had reached my limit, and this poor kid literally became the punching bag upon which I unleashed all my hurt and anger. Blow after blow, I just kept swinging and hitting his face with my fists. The whole scene felt dreamlike, but it was reality. I was so out of control that this poor kid had to go to the emergency room.

The next day at school, I pretended like nothing happened. But when the police came and arrested me, it set off a chain reaction of consequences that would send me in a downward spiral. I was expelled from school. And with nothing but time on my hands, I began hanging out with my cousins who, unlike everyone else, thought that my sending that kid to the hospital was the right thing to do.

Then they said something to me that struck a nerve: "Good job, little Homie! You're a down little Homie." This meant they were proud of me. It was something I had been looking for and didn't even realize it. Their praise felt good and soon would be something I craved and pursued.

The summer before high school, everything had been moving forward with my new gang association. I was feeling like these guys really had my back and that I was important to them. So I decided it was time to officially join the gang. This meant that I would be "jumped in." For me this involved four big guys surrounding me and then beating me. I felt punches all over my body. Someone focused on my face, while someone else hit me in the stomach, chest, and back. My natural inclination was to cover myself to try and protect my body, but it didn't help much, because once I fell to the ground, the kicking started. I was getting the full force of these guys as they gave me their no-holds-barred kicks, stomps, and punches. Then, just as I was beginning to think I wouldn't survive, it stopped. The beating was over, and they picked me up and began to hug me and praise me for not wimping out. Just like that, I was a gang member.

As you might imagine, my life went from bad to worse. I began smoking cigarettes, which quickly led to smoking weed. Soon came excessive drinking. With my negative experiences with the effects of alcohol, I should have wanted nothing to do with it. But because it was so prevalent, curiosity got the better of me.

Then came guns. Drugs and guns, as you might imagine, is a bad combination. But I had bought into the gang's brainwashing. They talked often about how everyone was out to get us and how we had enemies everywhere, but they were my family—and family takes care of family. Loyalty was king and demanded homage from all the gang's members.

Blinded, I was unable to see past their indoctrination. I had completely immersed myself in their way of life, soaking up the love—as misguided and warped as it was.

Life in the gang involved what we called "patrolling" the neighborhood. We would all take turns walking or driving around the neighborhood, our territory, looking for rival gang members while tagging our gang sign on buildings, walls, fences and bridges. This was our way of letting everyone know this was our 'hood, and they had better keep out.

We had guns stashed in certain areas around the neighborhood like homes, alleys, and cutouts in walls, just in case we needed to get to them in a hurry. We would "hit people up" while patrolling, asking strangers where they were from. Anyone we didn't recognize or who looked suspicious were fair game.

Once when we hit up a guy and asked him where he was from, he responded, "Nowhere, man. I don't bang."

He was telling us that he didn't belong to any gang, but suspicious by nature, I made him take off his shirt and prove that he didn't have any gang tattoos. He was terrified, because I was doing this while I pointed a gun at him.

I enjoyed making other people afraid. It gave me a sense of power. This was one of our main objectives in the gang. Making people afraid of us was what gave us the power to control others. This way they would do what we said when we said, or they would pay the consequences.

I remember another night we got caught "slippin' " (relaxing with our guard down), while we were patrolling the neighborhood. Some rival gang members drove up and we immediately threw up our gang signs as the car passed. But the car stopped, and three guys got out with guns drawn. As gunfire erupted, we immediately ran down a nearby alley, looking for a hideout. We did not have guns with us and were in between locations where we had guns stashed. We made it out that night unharmed, but we wouldn't be so lucky a few nights later.

A group of us, all high on crack, were at a friend's house when a rival gang rolled up and opened fire. We all ran and tried to duck for cover, but two of my homeboys got shot. That was the last time I would ever get caught slippin'. From that moment on I vowed that my "roll dog" or I would always carry a gun. We wanted to show no kind of weakness, not to mention that we didn't want to die.

Another part of gang life involved dressing to impress. We all took pride in looking good. We called it being "G'd up from the feet up." I had a size 36 waist and I would wear a size 50 in pants. My shirts were XXXL. A shaved head was mandatory. This explains why we never were able to hide from the cops. They knew what we looked like, they knew how we dressed, and they knew what our routines were. We would be pulled over and searched by the gang units two and three times a day. If they didn't find any drug paraphernalia or weapons, they would let us go. But they would document every time they stopped us.

Little did I know that all the police contact I had later would be used against me in court to prove that I was an active gang member. While I was in the gang I didn't care about that. I viewed it as part of the gang mystique. We were naïve enough to think we could either outsmart the cops or that we could handle doing a couple months or years in prison if they were able to make the charges stick.

Another aspect of daily gang life was competing to see how many girls in the neighborhood we could be with. Most of the girls in the neighborhood knew who we were and what we were about. Some girls kept their distance because they didn't want to get caught up in our lifestyle and become collateral damage. But there were plenty of other girls who liked the attention, the money, the drugs, and the parties. And everyone knew that girls in the 'hood partied for free.

By the age of fourteen I was smoking weed every day. Eventually that turned into "coco puffs," a combination of weed and crack. By the age of sixteen everyone in my generation had become full-blown tweekers, addicted to meth.

Another big part of the older gang members' daily routine was finding new recruits, usually adolescent kids who were looking for love (in all the wrong places, literally). But first they had to be tested to see if they had what it took. This came in various forms, but it usually meant getting into fights and purposely going into enemy gang territory looking for trouble.

This was my life. Eventually this life got me expelled from school so many times that I would never see the inside of a classroom again—at least not as a student.

BEYOND THE GANG

CHAPTER 2

GOOD DOG, BAD DOG

Do not remember the sins of my youth,
nor my transgressions;
According to Your mercy remember me,
For Your goodness' sake, O Lord.
(Psalm 25:7–8)

I was in and out of juvenile hall from the ages of fourteen to eighteen.

When I arrived at the detention center for the first time, I was escorted there by police and admitted through a secure entrance. The admittance procedure typically included the removal of handcuffs and the confiscation of shoes, belts, jewelry, and other personal items. Once that was completed, I passed through a security check that usually involved a thorough pat down and some form of metal detection. After general information was taken, I was forced to strip down naked and shower in front of several officers, after which I was issued a jumpsuit, assigned to a room, and given bedding. Not everyone had a cellmate; it depended on how full the detention center was.

A typical day in juvenile detention depends on the facility. The one I was regularly in and out of had its own daily schedule. Most days began with having to make our beds and get dressed. Then we would eat breakfast and clean our rooms for inspection. After that classes would begin and last several hours each day. After the school sessions there were groups to attend, like drug and alcohol group, family intervention training, or anger management. After dinner, there would be some supervised leisure activities, but for the most part it was free time. The days were extremely structured, with set times for morning release from rooms for breakfast, school, bathroom breaks, lunch, free time, dinner, visiting hours, mandatory showers, and bedtime.

In and out of juvie was the new normal for me, and to be honest I liked it. It sounds strange that someone would like being locked up in a detention center, but one of the main reasons I liked it was the structure and stability it provided. Having a daily routine that I could count on helped me emotionally, and it actually taught me some valuable lessons about planning and organization.

Fast-forward to just before my nineteenth birthday. I was expecting to be transferred out of juvenile detention to county jail to finish out my sentence, which should have been the natural transition. Instead I was released. I never found out whether it was a mistake, whether the jails were overcrowded, or whether it was some other reason, but I wasn't about to argue with this turn of events in my favor. I took advantage of my newfound freedom and made the decision to fully immerse myself in gang life. I wanted to live *mi vida loca*.

Because I was a leader in the gang, my return was seamless. I took on the responsibilities of recruiting new gang members and enforcing gang rules. I was respected, trusted, and most importantly, feared. My mission during this time was to cause as much havoc as I could and to let people know not to mess with me, my gang, or my girl.

When it came to girls I was no Casanova, but I did cycle through some girlfriends. I really wasn't interested in most of them. They were just around for fun, and that was okay with me because I wasn't looking for anything serious. That is, until the day I saw Alma. Even though I tried to play it cool around her, I was definitely captivated.

I met Alma before I went into juvenile detention for the last time. Because we had spent a little time getting to know each other before I went in, she often would write me letters while I was inside. As our friendship grew, I decided to ask her to be my girl right before I was released.

I tried to act indifferent by telling her, "Hey, if you want to be my girl that's cool. But if not, I can't make any commitments." Who was I kidding? It wasn't like I had any real prospects or even potential prospects. I was just playing the game.

To the gang I was important. To the younger gang members, my life looked good. The reality was that my life continued to spiral out of control. Juvenile detention had done nothing to rehabilitate me; it had only given me a place to live where I didn't have to worry about the normal day-to-day cares and concerns of life. On the outside all that was gone. Gang life had me addicted to crack and meth and led me to steal to feed my addiction. I had to have my next fix to function, and I would do whatever I had to do to score some drugs. I was headed for trouble.

The interesting thing about my downward spiral was that I kept running into Kobie's mom. I could not escape her. Every time I would see her, she would say things to me like, "God has a plan for your life, Gabriel" or "God loves you, Gabriel."

I liked her and didn't want to be disrespectful to her, so I would always respond by saying, "I know He does, Mrs. Mary." But in the back of my mind I couldn't help thinking, "How could He love me when I live like this?"

My downward spiral was about to reach rock bottom.

I remember December 30, 2001 like it was yesterday. I was hanging out with a friend and said, "Yo, take me to Santa Ana to score some drugs."

Before I went out that night my mom said to me, "Don't go out tonight. Stay home, son."

I don't know whether she had a sense about what would happen that night, but her pleading began to unsettle me. When I opened a can of beer, and it exploded all over me. It was as though someone or something was trying to get my attention. I was even beginning to think that maybe I should just stay home.

But I quickly and easily shook off those thoughts because my desire for drugs outweighed any logic in my mind that told me something didn't feel right about that night.

While my friend and I were driving around trying to score drugs, I saw a guy by the side of the road and thought, "Not in my neighborhood."

If I didn't know someone and they were in my neighborhood, they had better move on or things would get ugly. I tapped my friend on the shoulder and said, "Pull over so I can hit him up."

I jumped out and challenged him. "What's up? Where you from, man?"

It was as if I lit a match. The situation caught fire as he pulled out a gun. "Where am *I* from?" he shouted back. "Where are *you* from?"

We argued back and forth. Things seemed a little unpredictable, but at that moment I thought he was just using his gun as a prop, trying to look tough.

Suddenly I caught a glimpse of two of my friends coming around the street corner. I remember I asked one of them to give me his gun. I could tell that he didn't want to do it, probably because he could see that nothing good would come from it.

"If you don't give me that gun," I threatened, "I am going to beat you down."

He gave me his gun, and I decided to just shoot off one round in the air, assuming that once this guy saw that I had a gun and wasn't afraid to use it, he would calm down. Or even better, he would just take off.

This did not have the result I had hoped for. In fact it had the opposite effect. It seemed to have flipped a switch in his head, because he lost his mind and started firing his gun at me.

I was standing about twelve feet away from him when he began firing. Miraculously, not a single bullet hit me. While his bullets whizzed past me, I turned my gun on him and unloaded the entire magazine. I didn't miss. As soon as I saw him fall to the asphalt, I took off running.

Over the next few days, my mind raced in a thousand directions. I didn't know whether I had killed him. One thing I did know was that I had to lay low for a few weeks. I decided to stay at my parents' house until it all blew over.

About two weeks later, the police came pounding on the door at 5:00 a.m.

"Orange County Sheriff's Department! Open up! We have a search warrant."

Boom!

Before I could respond, they broke down the door with an entry ram. With guns drawn they yelled, "Gabriel Nieves! Gabriel Nieves!"

All I could think to say in that moment was, "I'm here! I'm here!"

Before I knew it they had jumped on me, their knees digging deep into my back. Several of them forced my face to the floor while another yanked my arms behind my back and handcuffed me. The officers had worked together like a NASCAR pit crew, and everything was over in under one minute.

I tried to play dumb as they took me away, pleading, "What's this all about?"

Even when we arrived at the county jail, I kept pretending. "Why am I here? I didn't do anything!"

When it came time for my one phone call, I called Alma. "They got me," I said. "I'm arrested."

I think the news hit her hard. She was in shock. And I was in shock, too. I told her I loved her and said I would be in touch soon.

Gang life was rough, but jail was a whole different animal. In county jail I had to put on a façade that I was hard core. I found myself saying things like, "Awe man, they ain't got nothin' on me" or "Doing time is a piece of cake, man."

I concluded that even if they locked me up for a few years, I would be okay. I would just run with all my Homies from juvie. There were so many people that I knew. As I used to say, "So many familiar faces, just with bigger cases."

My new accommodations gave me time to contemplate my situation. I calculated in my own mind that if they had a case against me, I probably would get fifteen years. So I began to resign myself to this number and even thought to myself, "I can do fifteen no problem. I'll do my time, be thirty-five when I get out. No biggie. I'll go upstate, get tatted up, and if my girl waits for me, great. If not, no big deal." I was trying to convince myself that everything would be fine.

Then I got a rude awakening when I went to court and met with my court-appointed attorney for my arraignment. In my mind I thought I'd make a plea deal. I told my public defender, "Hey, you get me a plea deal and I will sign for fifteen years right now!"

I was cocky, overconfident, and unrealistic. Then life got real serious, real fast.

My public defender looked me in the eye and handed me the court paperwork. "Do you see these charges here?"

The court document read, ATTEMPTED MURDER AND ILLEGAL USE AND POSSESSION OF A FIREARM.

"The state of California will give you a life sentence for these. Gabriel, you need to wake up. You are going to spend the rest of your life in jail. . . . So get comfortable. You're going to be in for a very long time."

When you hear that you're going to spend the rest of your life in jail, it does something to you, no matter how "bad" you think you are, how tough you pretend to be, or whether you've spent time in prison before. Fifteen years? I could do that. But the thought of life in prison, the thought of never getting out again, felt like being punched in the stomach. It was hard to breathe. My whole world just got smaller, and I felt everything closing in on me.

Going back to my cell that afternoon I was a stressed-out mess. I had been given a sack lunch that day. I was big boy and never skipped a meal. I liked to eat. But even if it had been filet mignon inside that sack, my stomach was so tied up in knots that the last thing I wanted to do was eat.

My chances of getting out seemed hopeless now. I was feeling defeated, like a cornered animal I did anything I could think of in an attempt to get out of this position. I started calling Alma and pleading with her. "Get me a new lawyer! Bail me out! You gotta help me get out of here!"

It was unfair and impractical to place so much pressure on her. She had no way to get me a new lawyer or pay my bail.

Everything I had taken for granted was about to be taken from me, forever. I was not even twenty-one. I had never been married. I had no kids. I didn't even have my driver's license. I no longer would be able to spend time with my little brothers, my family, or my girl. I was missing things I had never experienced. I felt sorry for myself.

I also realized that in prison, if someone shows even the slightest sign of weakness, they become the prey. I needed to focus on the fact that I was a respected member of a gang, and I needed to represent that to stay connected and protected.

A couple of days later I was heading back to my cell when I saw a guy coming my way with a Bible in his hand. I had seen guys reading their Bibles in the joint before. I thought they were weak and hypocritical, and I often made fun of them: "Oh what, now that you got caught and are forced to live in jail, you find God? Man, who are you kidding? You are just hiding behind God, using Him as some sort of crutch."

I always said that if one of those guys came to me and tried to talk to me about God, I'd let them have it. And one of them was coming my.

Innocently enough he said, "Hey man, God loves you."

"You have got to be kidding me, man. God doesn't love me. God can't love someone like me. I am about to get sentenced to life in prison. God ain't interested in someone in my situation."

Then he had the nerve to come back at me. "Well, you never know," he said, "God just might change your situation."

Clearly he had lost touch with reality. He didn't get it. He didn't know why I was there. If I couldn't change my situation, then God definitely wouldn't be able to change my situation.

"God doesn't hear people like me," I told him point-blank. "Listen, Homie, you are probably here for a parking ticket or something. Look, I gave my life to Jesus when I was thirteen years old. Look where that got me."

The next thing he did was share with me the biblical story of the prodigal, or reckless, son. The story is found in Luke, chapter fifteen, and in that chapter is the story of a son who took his inheritance and then went out and lived a crazy, reckless, party lifestyle. Spending all his money on wild parties and fast living left him broke. All his friends abandoned him, and he was forced to eat pig slop. He hit rock bottom, but in that moment of despair he came to his senses. He went back home to his father to beg forgiveness and work as a hired servant, only to be met with his forgiveness. Then his father threw a lavish party in his honor. When the father's eldest son asked the reason for such a celebration for his wasteful and wayward brother, the father responded, "For this son of mine was dead and is alive again; he was lost and is found" (verse 24 NIV).

Then this guy said one more thing that completely rocked me: "God has a plan for your life."

I thought of Mrs. Mary and every encounter I had with her in the neighborhood when she, too, spoke the same words of encouragement and told that God had good plans for me. Her words were based on a verse from Jeremiah: "For I know the thoughts that I think toward you, says the LORD, thoughts of peace and not of evil, to give you a future and a hope" (29:11).

No matter how far I ran, no matter where I went, I could not seem to outrun God. So, in a moment of indecision, I said, "Okay man, what do I do then? How do I get my life on track with God?"

He said, "You need to talk to God, and you need to ask God to help you. You need to repent and turn away from the gang life and turn your life toward God. You need to read your Bible." He handed me a Bible and continued, "You need to get to know Jesus, because He wants to do something big in your life."

He told me to start reading the gospel of John and as soon as I got back to my cell. I hopped in my bunk and opened up the Bible he gave me. Then I began soaking up the words of life. I never saw that guy again. But he left me with one thing I will never forget when he said, "Gabriel, I want to tell you something. This decision comes with a spiritual battle."

Of course I thought he was speaking of a physical battle. After all, I was in prison, which has its fair share of battles. "Yeah, I hear you, man. I know it's a dangerous place in here."

"No man," he responded. "A spiritual battle is going on inside your heart. Look, Gabriel, there are two packs of dogs inside of you, good dogs and bad dogs. Which pack do you think is going to win?"

"Oh man, that's easy," I answered. "The good dogs."

"Nope."

"Oh, okay. I get it. The bad dogs."

"No, Gabriel. It's the dogs you feed the most. They are the ones that will win."

CHAPTER 3
FREE AT LAST

Therefore, if anyone is in Christ, he is a new creation;
old things have passed away;
behold, all things have become new.
(1 Corinthians 5:17)

Life had new meaning for me now. This time my decision to follow Jesus was real, because I was committed to see it through. I might have been locked up, but I had a new-found peace in my life, and that peace even extended to my circumstances.

I stopped asking God to get me out of prison and began asking Him to simply help me out. I wanted God to help me follow Him. Even though my circumstances didn't change, I noticed that I began to change.

My language changed. I stopped swearing.

My mindset changed. I stopped looking at inappropriate things.

My heart changed. I stopped thinking evil about everyone and everything and began thinking good thoughts.

I couldn't wait to talk to Alma and share with her what had happened. I began telling her about God and speaking words of light and life to her. I had spent enough time speaking empty words of darkness to her and around her, but no more.

To say she was shocked is an understatement. She knew what I was like. She had been with me long enough to know my language, my attitude, and my behavior. The way I was talking to her now was completely different because I was completely different.

I was a changed man. I was born again.

I didn't care what happened to me. I was going to follow God and live for Jesus.

I tried to find ways to just live out my faith, even in my restricted life behind bars. I wanted to be a doer of the Word, as James 1:22 says: "But be doers of the word, and not hearers only, deceiving yourselves."

I began to look at people differently and started to love people instead of hating them. I wanted them to experience the joy that I now had. As you might imagine, most people in prison didn't want to hear it. They looked at me differently—even those I had been arrested with and was close to. They would listen to me say things like "God is going to get us out of here" and just laugh.

I had been in prison for nine months when my faith was both tested and reassured. I went to court to meet with my public defender, who told me, "Gabriel, I have some good news."

"What, I am getting out?"

"Well, not that kind of good news, but just like you wanted, the district attorney is willing to offer you fifteen years."

"What? I thought you said you had good news."

"What are you talking about? You were the one who told me you wanted fifteen years and that if I could get you that offer, you would sign it immediately. So that's what I did. I got the D. A. to agree to fifteen years."

"Man, I don't know."

The drugs were out of my system and I was filled with something better than hallucinogens: the Holy Spirit. I did not want to take that deal of fifteen years. I told her about the change in my life. I shared it all with her, even saying, "You are going to be the mouthpiece for God. God is going to use you in my case."

She paused for a moment. Then she said dismissively, "Okay, Gabriel. I'll tell you what. Since it is late, go back tonight, think about what is being offered, talk to your family, and I will bring you back here tomorrow. We will decide then what to do, okay?"

I went back to the county jail, but I didn't talk to anyone. I didn't call my Mom. I didn't call Alma. I told no one about the offer that the district attorney had made. Instead

I called on God. I prayed, "God, if this is your will for my life, just give me the strength to sign that deal. Give me the strength to do the time. Just go before me and show me the way. I know I am guilty of everything they are accusing me of, so if this is my punishment, then I accept it. Your will be done."

I remember feeling a peace that night that surpassed all understanding or logic. Then as I was reading my Bible, I came across Psalm 91, which I read again and again until I went to court:

> Whoever dwells in the shelter of the Most High will rest in the shadow of the Almighty. I will say of the Lord, "He is my refuge and my fortress, my God, in whom I trust." Surely he will save you from the fowler's snare and from the deadly pestilence. He will cover you with his feathers, and under his wings you will find refuge; his faithfulness will be your shield and rampart. You will not fear the terror of night, nor the arrow that flies by day, nor the pestilence that stalks in the darkness, nor the plague that destroys at midday. A thousand may fall at your side, ten thousand at your right hand, but it will not come near you. You will only observe with your eyes and see the punishment of the wicked.

If you say, "The LORD is my refuge," and you make the Most High your dwelling, no harm will overtake you, no disaster will come near your tent. For he will command his angels concerning you to guard you in all your ways; they will lift you up in their hands, so that you will not strike your foot against a stone. You will tread on the lion and the cobra; you will trample the great lion and the serpent.

"Because he loves me," says the LORD, "I will rescue him; I will protect him, for he acknowledges my name. He will call on me, and I will answer him; I will be with him in trouble, I will deliver him and honor him. With long life I will satisfy him and show him my salvation." (NIV)

As I walked into the courthouse the next day, I was nervous about the uncertainty of my future. I also felt at peace about it, because I knew I had a new and lasting relationship with God and that whatever happened to me, I would be okay with God on my side.

When I saw my public defender walking toward me, I was not expecting the greeting she gave me. She began throwing every foul word imaginable at me, saying, "They took the deal off the table! The district attorney's witnesses are showing up. We are going to trial."

"Oh, no we're not," I said, a bit combatively. "You'd better go back in there and get me those fifteen years."

"There is nothing I can do, Gabriel. They took the deal off the table. Now get dressed. We are picking the jury right now."

I knew I had prayed for God's will the night before, but I honestly didn't think going to trial would be God's will for me. I was forced to reconcile my thoughts and expectations of how I thought God would work with the reality of how He was working in the here and now.

I knew I shot this guy, and I couldn't deny it. If I was called to testify, I would have to admit that I did it. And if I admitted I shot him, I would get life in prison. There was no doubt of that.

The trial came the following week. During the three days of testimony, the state had everything they needed. They had eye witnesses and sworn testimony. They had everything they needed to convict me. It was an open-and-shut case, with or without my testimony.

As it came time for closing arguments the district attorney hit hard. Summarizing what he said in my own words, this is what I heard that day:

"Look at the defendant, Mr. Nieves, sitting over there. He looks good today, doesn't he? He is wearing a nice suit and tie. His hair is neat and combed, and he is looking respectable and presentable today. But do not be fooled by his outward appearance. What you see here in this courtroom today is not the real Mr. Nieves."

"This is the real Mr. Nieves," he said, pointing to a huge poster of me without a shirt on, covered in gang tattoos, with a shaved head. "The gang member in this picture, that is the real Mr. Nieves, the one who shot this poor victim and tried to kill him. This lifelong criminal, who has been in and out of the system for years, deserves to be in prison for the rest of his life."

Those were the final words and that was the final image the jury had before going to deliberate. When they left I leaned over and told my public defender, "I want to thank you for everything you did. I know you did the best you could for me. My fate is in God's hands now, and His will be done. God bless you."

As the bailiff took me from the courtroom, he said, "Chin up, champ. No news is good news. The longer they take to deliberate, the better it is for you. Hope for the best."

I took his words to heart. "Yeah? Okay, thanks. That's good advice. I will remember that."

In less than two hours the jury was back. They had reached a verdict.

My heart raced while the same bailiff who escorted me down brought me back up. This time he had nothing to say. He knew as well as I did there were no more words of encouragement to be offered. We both knew it did not look good for me.

He put me in a four-by-four cell in the court room and instructed me to wait here while the judge and jury were summoned.

In that moment God broke me.

I had already given my life to God, but He had truly brought me to a place of complete and total surrender. I fell to my knees in this clear box in the middle of the court room, and I began to weep.

I cried and I cried out to God, "I am scared, Lord. I know I am guilty. I confess to you all my sins. And even though I don't deserve it, I ask for your mercy. Please give me another chance. I am a changed man. You have changed me, and I am yours."

With hands raised, I finished by asking God for the strength to handle whatever came my way. I opened my eyes and looked at the wall in front of me. Someone had etched a Scripture verse, Isaiah 52:12, into the wall: "The LORD will go before you."

Sitting back at the defense table, this time handcuffed to it, the judge began. "Has the jury reached a verdict?"

"Yes we have, Your Honor."

"Please hand me your decision."

The judge silently read the words, pausing a moment to look at me and then at the jury. "On count two, the State of California, with regards to street terrorism, finds the defendant, Gabriel Nieves, guilty."

All I could do was bow my head and pray silently, "God, please have mercy on me."

Then the judge continued. "On count one, the State of California, with regards to attempted murder . . ."

He paused.

"God," I prayed, "please touch one person on that jury. Just one."

"On count one, the State of California, with regards to attempted murder, finds the defendant g—"

"Your Honor!" came a loud voice from the jury box.

What was going on? The juror, standing up, had just interrupted the judge before he could finish the word *guilty*!

"Your Honor, I do not know what is happening to me right now," the juror said, "but something is piercing my heart, and I cannot let you convict this young man of this crime."

"It's Jesus!" I shouted. Everyone told me to shut up, and I did. I didn't want to be held in contempt of court.

My public defender looked at me. "That lady just saved your life," she said.

"No, she didn't. *Jesus* just saved my life."

The judge, visibly annoyed, jumped in. "What do you mean, 'something is touching your heart'? Didn't you just spend two hours deliberating this case with eleven other jurors and come to a verdict?"

"Yes, Your Honor, but I was forced to cast my vote that way. It is not how I feel, and I cannot let this happen."

The judge was dumbfounded. "I don't know what to do. I have been a judge for over twenty years, and this has never happened to me before. I have had guilty verdicts, not guilty verdicts, hung juries, and mistrials. But I have never, ever, had a juror change their mind after the verdict was in." Pausing as if to set his thoughts in order, the judge declared, "My decision is that you will all go back into the jury room and see if you all can convince this juror of the evidence presented and change her mind. Until then, we are in recess."

The solidifying bang of his gavel echoed through the courtroom.

"All rise."

With that, the judge and jury left the room.

After two days of further deliberations, the verdict came back. It was a hung jury, eleven to one. God heard my prayer, or maybe He was giving me a momentary glimpse into what He was going to do by moving one juror the way that He did.

Either way, God touched this juror and she could not be swayed. God was for me. My response to His mercy was that I became a bold witness for Him. I was being held in the tank with about sixty other inmates, and I was determined to make sure that every single person who came into the tank heard about Jesus.

During this time I was reading about the apostle Paul. I saw in him someone who had been radically saved and became a radical witness for Jesus. Paul, who at one time was a killer of Christians, became the greatest witness for Christ. That motivated me even more. When I read about Paul's life, I wanted to be like him. Paul wrote in 1 Corinthians 11:1, "Imitate me, just as I also imitate Christ," so that is what I did.

Since I knew and had personally experienced God answering prayer, I started a prayer circle in the tank. It began with ten guys, and we would pray for each other and for God to do great things in our lives.

God was moving so powerfully that in a short time, the entire tank was praying together, more than sixty hardened criminals of various ethnicities were holding hands: gang bangers, drug dealers, you name it. They all were there. And God had us all praying together.

I was so willing to talk about God with anyone and everyone that I earned a nickname in prison: Gabriel the evangelist.

I knew that God was going to get me out, and all I wanted to do in the meantime was simply please Him. I wanted to serve Him with my life and share what He did in my life and what He could do for others.

While I was in the county jail awaiting a second trial, I prayed for the Lord to bring someone into my life to disciple me. I had so many questions about my faith and was like a sponge, absorbing every drop of truth and knowledge I came across.

One night while I was evangelizing in the tank, a guy named Michael said, "Hey, you really believe this Jesus stuff, huh, Homie?"

"Absolutely my friend!" I replied.

He was supposedly in custody doing "weekend time." Out of nowhere he told me that he had someone he wanted me to talk to on the phone. I thought he wanted me to pray for someone or something, so of course I agreed. He got on the pay phone and after the call went through, he called me over. "Here, Homie, talk to her."

"Nah man," I said. "I got a girl. It's cool."

"It's not like that. She's one of you."

"One of me?"

"Yeah," he said. "She's a hard-core Christian like you."

I picked up the phone. "Hi. This is Gabriel."

I was immediately greeted by the sweetest voice possible. "Hi, my name is Jerry. Michael has been telling me all about you and about how bold you are with your faith."

"I feel a little like Daniel in the lion's den at times," I told her, "but God has been protecting me."

"Can I send you a study Bible?"

"Sure, that would be awesome. Thanks!"

This was an answer to my prayer. After all, I had just asked the Lord for someone to disciple me, and little did I know that discipleship at this point would come in paperback form. A week later I remember the guard calling my name for a package. Inside was a study Bible along with a commentary by Pastor Chuck Smith.

Jerry had written a little note that she placed on the inside cover: "If you have any questions regarding the Bible, please feel free to ask me, and I will do my best to send you answers or other commentaries and Bible studies to help answer your questions."

I began to really grow spiritually during this time, and Jerry, better known as Mama Jerry, was greatly used by God to help me grow. I started receiving weekly packages with Bible studies that kept me digging deep into the Word of God.

My second trial date was approaching, and Alma and I were stressed out. I asked Mama Jerry if she would call Alma and invite her to church. I did not know what church she went to at the time, but I knew that she had a strong faith, so the church she attended must be pretty good.

Honestly I was surprised when Alma agreed to go to church with Mama Jerry, and it didn't take long before Alma's life was dramatically changed too. She was going to church, serving God, and loving every minute of her newfound faith and newfound family of faith.

It seemed that God not only was working and touching me, but He was touching those I loved as well.

I kept telling Alma, "Hey, I'm going to get out! I just know I'm going to get out. Look at what God has done with my case. And when I get out, I want to come home to you as my wife."

I knew it was a big risk. Asking from prison after having been locked up now for several years was not the storybook way to propose. I knew we hadn't been able to spend much time together because of my situation, but I also knew she was the one.

She needed some time to pray about it and seek God's direction.

Alma says,

> *You are probably asking yourself, "Why did she wait all those years for Gabriel?" And to be honest I cannot give you an answer to that question, other than I loved him. As illogical and unwise as a relationship with a known gang member sounds, I still loved him.*
>
> *It all began when I was sixteen years old. Gabriel and I had already been friends for a while before we started dating. As I look at the genesis of our relationship, a passage from the book of Genesis comes to mind. Joseph, after being sold into slavery by his brothers, eventually rose to a position of powerful*

leadership in the most powerful country in the world at that time. He looked at his brothers, who were at his mercy, and declared, "As for you, you meant evil against me, but God meant it for good" (Genesis 50:20).

Meeting Gabriel could have been one of those dysfunctional and devastating relationships that destroyed me. And I have no doubt that the enemy of God intended to destroy both Gabriel and me. Instead, God used my relationship with Gabriel to bring me to salvation.

Now, that is the good news, but our relationship prior to that was not filled with much that was good. I wish I could tell you that Gabriel was the perfect boyfriend (I would have even settled for a decent boyfriend), but the fact is that he was a horrible boyfriend. He never was consistent in our relationship. He would never call when he said he would call. He would leave me waiting for him when we would make plans to go out. When his drug addiction started to get worse, he would go missing for weeks, sometimes months, before resurfacing in my life. Inevitably, every time I was ready to leave him and move on because I got tired of waiting, he would call or turn up again. Gabriel's life really was all about *the gang and spending time with his home-boys, and most of our dates ended up with our hanging out at a house in his neighborhood with all of them.*

To give you one example of how disappointing he could be at times, Gabriel had promised to take me out to celebrate my eighteenth birthday. On my big day, he never showed up, and he did not even bother to call and say happy birthday. The reality was that Gabriel was usually drunk or high. He always had a weapon on him, and most of the time he was just a jerk to people around him, always looking for someone to challenge him so he could simply beat them down. He was pretty mean, but most of the gang members were that way. Life was all about them, and nothing and no one else mattered.

Why I allowed him to treat me that way puzzled even me. I was doing well in school and was going to be the first person in my family to not only graduate high school but go on to college. I had good grades, I had plans for my life, and I was not going to be held back by the neighborhood or anyone from it. My only explanation as to why I did not leave Gabriel when he treated me so poorly was that I grew up being rejected by my own father. So somewhere in life's journey I began to think that was normal. Then a little further down the line, I accepted that it was just how guys were.

I did not understand that I was supposed to be treated better than that, and I certainly never knew that in God's eyes, I had great worth and value and that being treated as a lady, with respect and love, was just the beginning.

There were times, however, when it was just Gabriel and me, and he would show some other emotions besides anger. He talked about his dreams of getting married to me, having children, and being a family. I think in his mind it was more like a fantasy. It was something he wished for, but because of his gang lifestyle he knew it would never happen. For me it was actually the other way around. I knew one day that I would get married to Gabriel. What I didn't know was how we would actually get there and how God would work it out in such a way that I not only would be willing to marry him but would truly desire that.

Before things got better, however, they got worse. I remember the phone call from Gabriel on December 31 in the middle of the night. A phone call so late at night honestly did not surprise me. He would often call in the middle of the night after he got drunk or high. This time was different. He called again and again, leaving messages for me to pick up the phone. Finally I picked up, and for the first time ever saw Gabriel in a completely different way. He told me how he shot someone and that he was scared. He was being vulnerable and had genuine remorse for what he had done. He even cried, which was something I had never seen him do before. When he called me nine days later and told me he had been arrested, I knew he was going away for a long time.

When I first visited Gabriel, I knew I had a choice to make: either I was going to stay with him and be there for him during this time, or it was time for me to move on with my life. Finally this was my way out, I thought. I could now move on with my own dreams and be free of this horrible relationship. But I soon realized that Gabriel had no one. His family abandoned him, although the reality was they abandoned him long ago. But this time they were quick to write him off as a lost cause. So against my better judgment, I decided to be there for him. There was a part of me that felt sorry for him and didn't want him to have to face all of this alone. Little did I know that this decision not only would change my future, but it would change my eternity.

The first months after Gabriel was arrested, he was a complete basket case. He was stressed out, anxious, and edgy. He would say things like, "If you love me, you'll find a way to bail me out." I was eighteen years old and had no money, connections, or contacts. I had no lawyer friends. I had nothing that could help Gabriel in his current situation.

Then about three months after his arrest, I started seeing a difference in Gabriel. He was no longer asking me to help get him out. He suddenly had peace and joy that I had never seen in him before. It did not matter that he was behind bars facing some serious jail time. Gabriel continued to change, and that change was obvious to all. With his change came a change in our letters, phone calls, and visitations. They were all centered on God. Gabriel couldn't stop talking about how God could do the impossible, how God could change his circumstances, and how God was changing his heart. I knew Gabriel was really changing, because he even started sharing with me not only what was happening to him but how I should make changes, like not saying bad words or drinking any longer. He encouraged me to read the Bible so I could experience what he was experiencing, and he began encouraging me to go to church.

I was always quick to remind Gabriel that I was Catholic, so I believed in God and went to Mass occasionally, but I really did not want to become this super religious person. I knew that Gabriel was praying for me, and he kept sharing God's Word with me every time we talked. Even though I was somewhat resistant on the outside, the Word of God started to take root in my heart.

I remember that my car radio was stuck on the local Christian station, and I would always seem to be driving when Pastor Greg Laurie was on. He was always talking about our eternal destination. I felt so convicted every time I heard him speak that I would pray the sinners prayer every time. After all, I did want to go to heaven. I was just conflicted about what that meant with regard to being raised Catholic and what I now saw in Gabriel.

After I turned nineteen, not much had changed. I believed Jesus was God and Savior, but I wasn't living for Him. He was not Lord of my life. During this time, one of the ways I dealt with all that was going on in my life was to really focus on my studies. I would go to work, then to school, and then go home and do homework. Then I would get up the next day and do it all over again. From Friday to Sunday I would visit Gabriel at the county jail.

During this time Gabriel's first trial had happened, and God had shown Himself strong on his behalf. Gabriel's faith was only ignited more, and he was sure God was going to get him out of that jail cell. He started talking to me about getting married and how when he was released, he wanted to come home to a wife and not to a girlfriend. I was only 19. Though I loved Gabriel and had no doubt of his change or that I wanted to be married to him, I was a little uncertain about how things were going to work out. As much as we thought he was going to get out of jail, he was still in prison after all. Also, I knew my mom and brother would be disappointed by my choice, and I would have to give up my dream wedding. After much prayer and consideration, I decided to go through with the marriage. So, I made the arrangements.

I knew from the very beginning that Alma was the one for me. There was always something different and unique about her and our relationship, and I could not have been happier when she said yes to my proposal.

On May 3, 2003, we got married.

Eventually the district attorney made good on her promise to bring charges against me once again. This time around I hired my own attorney. I was ready.

There was an additional force on my side: Mama Jerry and her prayers. The week before the trial, Mama Jerry asked if she could attend. I was concerned because she was a little white lady from the South, and I honestly didn't want to expose her to all the gory details of my gang life and the related gang shooting. But I agreed. After all, it was Mama Jerry. How could I say no to her?

Day after day she came and sat in the same seat in the courtroom. I would glance back at her periodically during the trial and see her simply sitting there, praying to God. After the trial she told me that during one of the breaks the district attorney asked her if she was a reporter. She replied, "Oh no, dear, I'm here for moral support for my brother Gabriel. I'm here praying for him."

The result of the trial was that this time around, even though I was found guilty, I was sentenced to four years in jail and credited with time served. I had been in prison for more than three years at this point. After doing the math, the judge determined I had four more months to serve, but he wasn't going to let me serve it out where I had been. He was sending me upstate to finish my time at Wasco State Prison.

Not Wasco.

I knew there were some bad dudes up there, lifers who didn't care about anyone or anything. Murderers and rapists and the worst of the worst in life were there. And what did these guys have to lose? They already had lost their freedom. Many would never see the light of day again, and that changes a person. For the already hardened criminal, it often makes them even more violent and determined to cause havoc.

I had asked God for one more chance, and I knew in my heart that He was giving it to me. Four months wasn't that long, but I didn't see why I had to go to Wasco. I had a good thing going where I was. I was witnessing to other inmates and praying with them. Why did God want to stop this work?

I would soon see why God was sending me to Wasco State Prison.

After getting to Wasco and spending a few days in that hellhole, I believe God showed me what my life would be like if I went back to my old way of living. God used this time to once and for all get rid of any lingering taste I might have had to return to gang life. God wanted to make sure that when I got out, I had no desire whatsoever to live as I had once lived, to do what I once did, or to be who I once was. This was God's way of lovingly warning me.

I took that warning to heart, and on August 4, 2004, I was set free.

CHAPTER 4
THE ROAD TO RECONCILIATION

"Do not remember the former things,
Nor consider the things of old.
Behold, I will do a new thing."
(Isaiah 43:18–19)

Life on the outside not only gave me a fresh start, but it also helped me appreciate things in a fresh way. The first thing I wanted to do was go to church. Mama Jerry had taken Alma to church at a place called Calvary Chapel Costa Mesa, so of course I wanted to go there.

I hated it almost immediately. As soon as we walked in, I wanted to turn around and walk back out. The building was a throwback to the seventies, with large ornate chandeliers, outdated carpet, and stuffy music. I didn't feel there were people in this place like me. In my mind, I felt as though I stood out like a sore thumb, and there was no way these old white people would be welcoming to someone like me. It was a complete culture shock.

Begrudgingly, I stayed that first day and agreed to give the church and the people a shot because Alma loved it so much, and it was the place Mama Jerry loved so much. Slowly, over the next few weeks, I began warming up to it. I couldn't deny there was something special about the senior pastor, Chuck Smith. Even though to me he was an old guy, he had a certain sparkle, an anointing that radiated from him and through his teaching.

Shortly after I began attending Calvary Chapel Costa Mesa, I met a guy named Tommy Cota. God led me to begin a friendship with him that is still going strong to this day. Through that friendship God would do something else I never expected.

One of the first things Tommy did was invite Alma and me to his house for something he called fellowship. I didn't even know what "fellowship" meant. I remember arriving at his house feeling a little nervous and thinking, "What is fellowship? What are we going to be doing?"

I quickly learned that fellowship basically meant spending time with other believers and sharing what God was doing in and through our lives. And I loved it. I thought, "Bring on the fellowship!"

The Lord also continued to use Mama Jerry in our lives. She took Alma and me under her wing and discipled us for about a year. One day when we were spending time with Mama Jerry, she prophesied over me, which was another first-time experience. She said, "Gabriel, you will be a pastor one day, standing behind a pulpit sharing the gospel. And your wife will stay home and raise your babies."

I remember telling her, "Oh no, Mama Jerry. Alma will have to be the breadwinner for us. I have a criminal record. I'll never get the kind of job I need to take care of a family like that."

She smiled as if to say, "Oh Gabriel, you just wait and see."

I was adapting to my newfound church family and started serving anywhere I could, a little here a little there. I was happy just doing whatever needed to be done. It didn't matter whether I was taking out the trash, cleaning the bathrooms, or setting up tables and chairs. No job was too small.

Then unexpectedly one day, I felt the Lord prompting me to write down my story and turn it into a rap song. Loving rap music as I did, I began to write my story and put it to music. All the while I was on high parole, which meant meeting my parole officer twice a week. My parole officer even would come to my house to check up on me. He had me on a short leash and was just waiting for me to mess up. No doubt he thought it was only a matter of time before I made a mistake and he would take me off the streets and send me back inside.

Early after my release I also had to adapt to dealing with my old friends and gang members. It didn't take long after my release for my old friends to start calling. They wanted to know when I was going to rejoin the gang.

That was not going to happen. God had made it perfectly clear to me in Wasco what my fate would be if I returned to my old ways and my old friends. Instead I decided I would witness to them and invite them to church. As you might imagine, this did not go over well.

When I shared what God had done in my life, my former gang friends mocked me and said it would never last. When I shared what God could do in their lives, they laughed, and when I invited them to church, they rejected my invitations and dismissed it all as a phase I was going through.

Most of them reasoned they would just wait me out and that in a few weeks or maybe months, I would come to my senses and rejoin them. The irony was they were the ones who needed to come to their senses. They were still blind to the truth and rejected what they needed most: God.

As good as my new life was on the outside, it came with some hardships. Being a felon on parole made it extremely difficult to get a job. Everywhere I went, as soon as it came time for the background check, the interview was over before it really started. Then it was on to the next opportunity—that is until one day God put me in the right place at the right time.

An acquaintance at church told me about a job at a pool product business. He said, "Gabriel, go down there and apply, and just tell them I sent you."

So that is exactly what I did. I went down the next day and applied, mentioning who sent me. When it came time for the background check, I got called back to the owner's office. I thought, "Well, that was quick. I guess it's on to the next opportunity now that they know I'm an ex-con. This is over."

But that is not what happened. The owner had me sit down. Then he asked me one question: "Gabriel, are you done shooting people?"

I was quick to respond. "Absolutely, sir. I am so done with all that."

"Okay. Go grab a uniform and head to the warehouse. You start today.'"

I was surprised and immediately thanked God for the opportunity.

When I got to the warehouse, the supervisor handed me a broom and said, "Gabriel, we want you to sweep the entire warehouse."

Sweep is exactly what I did, and I did it with joy because I was so thankful to have a job. I knew that God tells us in Zechariah 4:10 not to despise the day of small beginnings, so I wanted to be faithful in even the smallest of jobs.

It took me two full days to sweep the warehouse. I went back to my boss and said, "Okay, I'm done. I swept the entire warehouse."

My boss looked shocked because, as I later found out, most people never finished the job. They usually quit after a few hours. It was my willingness to do whatever I needed to do that helped me move up in the company. Even though I was a former drug-using, gangbanging, ex-con, God graciously had His hand on my life.

I was blessed working at the pool supply business and was thankful for the opportunity. I worked hard not only because I wanted to do a good job, but also because I was motivated to move up in the company. I had survived the gang life and was out of prison. Everything finally seemed to be going well. Then one day I received a phone call from Alma.

She was hysterical and crying over the phone, telling me, "They came with guns! They came with guns!"

I told her to take a moment and gather herself and then tell me what had happened. My heart was racing, and I could feel myself getting worked up. Alma paused and took a few deep breaths. Then she told me what happened.

Two guys had come to the house looking for Christian, my brother-in-law's fifteen-year-old nephew. We had allowed Christian to stay at our house for a couple of weeks. Alma told the men, who were wearing gloves, beanies, and black jackets, that Christian did not live there.

They immediately pulled out the guns and told her, "We are looking for him, so make sure you tell him we'll be back!"

Alma told the men that we were Christians, that we didn't want any problems, and that it was a family home. This set one of the guys off, who told her, "I had a family until that dumb kid messed things up!"

Apparently Christian was playing Romeo with the man's wife.

By the grace of God, I was not home when this happened. All the feelings I thought were no longer inside of me began to slowly creep back. If I still had been a gang member, I would have retaliated like a gang member. It's as though the Devil himself was whispering in my ear, "How could you let these guys disrespect you this way?" I felt myself starting to listen to the lies inside my head. I wanted to call my old acquaintances for one last favor.

Then, in the mist of all my rage, I gently heard the whisper of the Holy Spirit telling me to call my friend Tommy instead. I knew Tommy was from the neighborhood and would understand where I was coming from. He might even go with me to handle these guys, I thought. Tommy's response was something I never expected.

As I began to tell him everything that just went down, he patiently listened until I was done. I knew could he hear in my voice how upset I was. After I finished, Tommy simply said, "Let's pray for the guy, bro."

I couldn't believe my ears. *Pray for the guy who flashed a gun at my wife? Are you kidding me, Tommy?* And then he said something I'll never forget: "How would you feel if a fifteen-year-old teenager messed with your wife?"

I couldn't believe he went there. I didn't have a response. All I could say was, "All right, man. You pray."

As soon as he began to pray, I felt my heart softening and Jesus reminding me that I was a new creation. It was at that moment that I felt as though I were on the Devil's Most Wanted list.

Shortly after everything settled down, we found out that Alma was pregnant with our first son. The thought of being a father was exciting and extremely nerve-racking for me. I was largely afraid because I had such a bad example of fatherhood in my stepdad and never knew my biological dad. I didn't want to blow it. I felt the pressure mounting, but I refused to be a deadbeat dad, and I refused to run and take the easy way out.

I knew what I had to do. I needed to go to God and ask Him for help, strength, and wisdom. This is where my friendship with Tommy also helped me move forward in my walk with God. One day while we were talking about fatherhood he said, "Gabriel, if you keep seeking Jesus, he will make you the father you want to be."

Tommy was right. Sure enough, over the years my heavenly Father has been showing me how to be a good father.

CHAPTER 5

FATHERLY WISDOM

A father to the fatherless . . .
is God in his holy dwelling.
(Psalm 68:5 NIV)

I love being a dad. Ever since our firstborn son came into this world, I have always wanted to be the best father I could be. Part of my motivation was that I never wanted my children to experience anything close to the same neglectful indifference I grew up with. My other motivation has been to be a reflection of my Father in heaven to my kids.

There is no distancing ourselves from the reality that fathers play an important role in the development of their children. Even though it is true that no earthly father is perfect, no earthly father has all the answers, and no earthly father has it all together. It is, however, true that when an earthly father decides to live a life that reflects his love and devotion to his heavenly Father, it impacts the lives of their children. It is so important to teach our kids how to live an abundant life by living according to God's Word.

When he was president of Princeton University, Woodrow Wilson emphasized this fact in remarks to a parent's group:

> I get many letters from you parents about your children. You want to know why we people up here at Princeton can't make more out of them and do more for them. Let me tell you the reason we can't. It may shock you just a little, but I am not trying to be rude. The reason is that they are your sons, reared in your homes, blood of your blood, bone of your bone. They have absorbed the ideals of your homes. You have formed and fashioned them. They are your sons. In those malleable, moldable years of their lives you have forever left your imprint upon them.[1]

We cannot neglect our responsibility to our children, and we cannot pawn off our responsibility to raise them on any one else or on any other organization.

---

1. As quoted in Tim Elmore, *Nurturing the Leader within Your Child* (Nashville: Thomas Nelson, 2001), 76.

It is not the duty of the church to raise godly kids. It is not the responsibility of the school teacher to instill morality and ethics into our children. It is the responsibility of every parent in every home everywhere to take ownership of the moral, ethical, and spiritual development of their children. And our heavenly Father has given us an example to follow and the all tools we need to help our kids grow in His grace.

Some of the ways in which God deals with us are ways we can as parents follow His example and reflect his nature. For example, God our heavenly Father corrects us when we begin to stray, when we begin to rebel, or when we drift from His word. God's discipline and always an extension of His grace and love, as Hebrews 12:5–6 says:

> "My son, do not regard lightly the discipline of the Lord, nor be weary when reproved by him. For the Lord disciplines the one he loves, and chastises every son whom he receives." (Hebrews 12:5–6 ESV)

As fathers, as parents, we need to help our children realize that correction is an extension our love and concern for them. When they begin to stray down paths that may be harmful, when they begin to rebel in ways that are dishonoring or disrespectful, and when they drift from the truth of how God wants them to live, correction needs to happen.

Parents, we need to train our children to recognize the ways in which God uses His Holy Spirit to correct us as we live out our daily lives. Understanding the conviction of the Holy Spirit and sensing those spiritual "nudges" that God gives to his children help us to respond and obey.

Our heavenly Father also provides for His children. For earthly fathers that provision goes beyond paying the bills, filling our kids' stomachs with food, and putting clothes on their backs, although it does include that. Showing our children all the different ways God provides for them will teach them to trust God and rest in His perfect timing. God knows what we need before we even ask Him (see Matthew 6:8) and God will supply every one of our needs "according to His riches in glory by Christ Jesus (Philippians 4:19).

So much worry, anxiety, and human effort is wasted because we can forget as Gods children that He has promised to take care of us and to provide for all our needs. As a parent, your example in this will help to reinforce God's loving, constant, and consistent provision in your child's heart and mind.

Our heavenly Father also provides us with spiritual wisdom. Fathers, encourage your kids to use their God-given gifts and talents, but also make sure they see that wisdom—true wisdom—comes from our heavenly Father. Help them to see that the Bible is the ultimate source of wisdom.

God invites us to tap into His wisdom whenever we need it and to run to Him when we don't know what we are doing and when we don't know how to respond. We need to demonstrate this to our kids, showing them that we turn to God when we don't have the answers, when we need His direction, and when we need clarity on how to proceed and respond in certain situations. Let them see you turn to God and ask for wisdom. Let them see how God provides that wisdom to His children like a good father (see James 1:5).

We must also never forget that God always stands ready and willing to take us back when we make mistakes. Forgiveness is an integral part of God's nature and character. He is the ultimate example of forgiveness, and as parents we need to be ready and willing to forgive our children when they make mistakes. Forgive them when they mess up, take them back when they go astray, and love them no matter the mistakes they have made, because God always stands ready to forgive all of our sins, big and small.

As a parent may you never have to endure the sleepless nights and heartache of a child who plunges headlong into sin, disregarding the loving instruction you gave and demonstrated to them. But if you do, stand ready to receive them back as God teaches us to do in the story of the prodigal son:

> "When he finally came to his senses, he said
> to himself, . . . "I will go home to my father
> and say, 'Father, I have sinned against both

heaven and you, and am no longer worthy of being called your son. Please take me on as a hired servant.' "

"So he returned home to his father. And while he was still a long way off, his father saw him coming. Filled with love and compassion, he ran to his son, embraced him, and kissed him. His son said to him, 'Father, I have sinned against both heaven and you, and I am no longer worthy of being called your son.'

"But his father said to the servants, 'Quick! Bring the finest robe in the house and put it on him. Get a ring for his finger and sandals for his feet. And kill the calf we have been fattening. We must celebrate with a feast, for this son of mine was dead and has now returned to life. He was lost, but now he is found.' " (Luke 15:17–24 NLT)

As we forgive our children (and they will give us plenty of opportunities to demonstrate forgiveness), we help give them a glimpse of God's forgiveness in their lives.

CHAPTER 6

A NEW SONG

For I know the thoughts that I think toward you,
says the LORD,
thoughts of peace and not of evil, to give you a
future and a hope.
(Jeremiah 29:11)

Serving in church and working at the pool products business kept me busy, but God was still moving me to continue writing music. I wrote songs whenever I could, wherever I could, and on whatever I could find. I even wrote on napkins while I was eating. I thought about what kind of music would get my attention and stop me in my tracks if I heard it playing somewhere. That was the kind of music I wanted to make.

Music had become an important part of how I shared what God had done in my life. I continued to write music as God kept putting a new song in my heart. I love what it says in Psalm 40:3: "He has put a new song in my mouth—praise to our God; many will see it and fear, and will trust in the LORD."

That was exactly what I wanted to do: praise God through song and see many people put their trust in Him. In 2005, I released my first CD, *The Message*, followed by *From the Neighborhood to Fatherhood* in 2006. The main verse for the second release came from 1 Corinthians 13:11: "When I was a child, I spoke as a child, I understood as a child, I thought as a child; but when I became a man, I put away childish things." That verse describes the change that God was doing in my life. I was done with the foolishness and immaturity of my youth and was growing into what I was meant to do.

During this time God had me cross paths with an old friend who had a connection in the music industry. I knew nothing about recording music and didn't know what went into studio time, mixing music, instrumentation, vocal tracks, or audio engineering. All I knew was that I wanted to rap for Jesus. I held on to the words of Psalm 37:5: "Commit your way to the LORD, trust also in Him, and He shall bring it to pass." And that is what God did. This connection helped me book my first recording session in a studio.

A real music studio! A real recording session! I was so nervous. Walking into the studio, I looked around and thought, "I have no idea what I am doing, but here goes nothing."

That day I recorded four songs. During the sessions the studio owner kindly showed me the ropes. He took the time to explain how the process worked, going over what was important to make quality music. I learned a lot that day.

Out of that session a CD was created, and I couldn't wait to hand copies out to my friends and family. Tommy one of the first people to get one of my CDs. I handed it to him and said, "I am rapping on this CD! Can you believe it, man? I hope you like it."

"Okay," he said. "I just hope it's not cheesy. There is so much cheesy Christian music that I've heard, and I hope this isn't one of those."

I thought, "What if it is cheesy?" I never thought about the fact that maybe what I liked actually sounded ridiculous to others.

A few days went by and I got a call from Tommy while I was at work. I thought, "This is the moment of truth. Tommy will tell me whether or not this music is good."

"Hey, Gabriel, I listened to your CD. . . and hey, it's not bad at all! In fact, I have a Bible study coming up. Would you do a few of your songs for it?"

Without thinking or hesitating I said, "Of course! I'm in."

After we hung up, I panicked. *What was I thinking? I have never stood up in front of people! How in the world am I going to sing songs in front of a group?* I began to get nervous. When the day eventually came, I sang my songs and made it through, as nerve racking as it was. I am sure it wasn't the best performance, but I'm glad I stepped out and did it.

To my surprise I began getting some calls the next day from people who wanted to book me to come and sing at their churches. All of a sudden I was performing at churches and my music was taking off. I had to decide what I was going to call my music ministry. I remember God impressing upon my heart, "What's more important, the messenger or the message?" And there it was. My music ministry had a name: The Message.

God continued to open doors for me to take His message and my music into a variety of locations. He has used those opportunities to grow me in my faith and in my confidence in speaking to crowds. And He has used it to grow me musically.

While my music was continuing to reach others and was getting some recognition, I connected with an artist named Popo Lopati. Popo and I decided to join forces and do music together. We bonded quickly and played lots of gigs. Then one day while we were talking, Popo asked me to share my testimony with him. As I was telling my story, I felt the Lord prompting me to ask Popo if he knew someone named Myron May (the man I shot). I was convinced there was no way they would know each other.

"Oh yeah," Popo said. "I know Myron. He's my nephew."

My heart sank. *His nephew? You have got to be kidding me, God!*

"So, how is Myron doing?" I asked casually.

"We need to pray for him," Popo told me. "He has been running with the wrong crowd, and a while back he got shot by some gang dudes. He needs some real help, Gabriel."

I thought, "How do I tell my friend that I was the one who shot his nephew? And what was that going to do to our friendship?" Because I felt God had prompted this discussion, I knew I needed to come clean.

"Listen, Popo," I said. "I need to tell you that I was the guy who got into the shootout with your nephew."

"No way." He could not believe it.

What I couldn't believe was how gracious Popo had been in seeing me for who I was and for not holding something from my past against me.

I thought our conversation had taken place for the purpose of immediate reconciliation with Myron, but Popo told me that he didn't think it was the right time. Myron was still heavily involved in the gang life. "Let's wait on Gods timing," he said. "His timing is always right."

God's timing arrived in the most unexpected of ways. A few months later I received a call from Popo's wife in the middle of the night. "Gabriel, please pray," she told me. "Popo is being taken to the hospital and he is currently unresponsive." Then she hung up.

I drove straight there, and when I arrived I walked into confusion. Popo's family and friends in the waiting room already were dealing with the news that he had died of a heart attack. That night I lost a good friend and partner in ministry.

At Popo's funeral, I was one of the pallbearers. Afterward I got a message on Facebook from the last person I had ever expected to hear from: Myron May.

"Hey, I know you know who I am," he wrote. "I want to tell you that I have been running from God for many years, and I cannot believe that someone I have despised and hated for so many years is so closely connected to me. I cannot believe how close you were to my uncle."

I was blown away. My first thought was that this had to be some sort of joke or even a plan for some revenge. But I took the chance, I responded to his message and we agreed to meet. We talked for hours, it was absolutely amazing and by God's grace the man I shot became my friend.

CHAPTER 7
DIAMONDS FROM DUST

I'll give you a new heart,
put a new spirit in you.
I'll remove the stone heart from your body
and replace it with a heart that's God-willed,
not self-willed. (Ezekiel 36:26–27 MSG)

I have always understood loyalty, and I believe that my upbringing and the gang culture contributed to the deep sense of loyalty that I have. The saying in a gang is that you need to be "loyal to the soil" (loyal until death), or you are not liked or respected. It was all or nothing in that life. I don't see it much differently now with my new life in Christ. When Jesus took hold of my heart, I gave Him the same loyalty I gave my gang, which was everything I had.

I remember a lot of old friends would call to check up on me and see what I was up to. Now my loyalty to Jesus has surpassed all other loyalties, even to my old friends from the 'hood. I still felt a certain loyalty to them, only that loyalty was to share Jesus with them. I wanted the best for them, and the best for them was God. I would share with them, invite them to church, and do whatever I could whenever I could to bring Jesus to them.

One day one of my old homeboys from the neighborhood called and started telling me I was just going through a phase and that sooner or later, I would be back to the neighborhood and running in the gang again.

I told him about how much I loved my Homies, but even better, how much God loved them. Then it felt as though the Holy Spirit took over and gave me an illustration to share with my friend. I said, "Homie, you out of everyone know me. You know how much heart I had in the gang. You know I was willing to die for the neighborhood! Remember every time I would come up with drugs, girls, guns, or cash? Tell me, where would I go?"

"The 'hood," he answered.

"That's right," I said. "The 'hood."

"I would share everything good I had with my Homies in the 'hood. Well, Homie," I said, "Ain't nothing changed! I've found something good. And as a matter of fact, He is more than good, and His name is Jesus Christ."

I wish I could say that conversation ended with my friend surrendering his life to God, but it didn't. It reminded me that no matter the cost, I was going to continue to share God with everyone He gave me opportunity to talk with. And it also reminded me of someone else from the neighborhood, and I wanted to find out what happened to him.

I began looking for Ivan, one of my closest Homies growing up. He had been sent to the California Youth Authority at the age of sixteen, and over time I lost contact with him. I would often pray for Ivan and ask the Lord to let me see him one more time so that I could share with him what God had done in my life.

God is so good and gracious. One day I did a search for him on social media. Someone popped up with the exact name, only this guy was out in the wilderness of Mexico and had the title of pastor. I thought there was no way this was my old homeboy from the 'hood, but when I saw the profile picture, I began to celebrate. It was him! My friend was a pastor in Mexico. I quickly connected with him, and the first time we talked on the phone, we spent hours sharing all the amazing changes God had made in our lives.

The story of how Ivan came to Jesus still brings tears to my eyes. He was one of the youngest kids in the gang, only thirteen when he got jumped in. I remember that day because I was the one who did it. Ivan was rejected by his mom, so he quickly found the love he was longing for in the gang. He would always call the older homeboys in the neighborhood his fathers. He was constantly in and out of juvenile hall and had built up quite a reputation there for being a fighter. His fighting is what eventually got him transferred out of juvenile hall to the California Youth Authority (today the California Department of Juvenile

Justice), which essentially was a maximum security facility for youth offenders. It was there that God took hold of Ivan's life.

Ivan was at the peak of his gang career. He was a "shot caller" in prison, well-respected and constantly in lock-down. One day there was an invitation for chapel, and Ivan signed up. He only did this to get out of his cell for a while and find out what the word was in the yard. Little did Ivan know that he had an appointment with God that day.

The pastor who spoke in chapel said, "Jesus loves you and can change the hardest of hearts." Then he asked a simple question, hoping the inmates would understand the love of God: "Who here would die and take a bullet for any of your Homies?"

He looked around and, to his surprise, no one raised a hand. He said it again. "I said, who here would die for any of your Homies?"

This time Ivan, with a wicked smirk, pridefully raised his hand. The pastor followed up with another question. "So you would be willing to die and take a bullet for your friends, huh?"

Without hesitation Ivan said, "Absolutely! And I know all my Homies would do the same for me!"

Then the pastor used those questions to explain to Ivan how Jesus did the same for him, how Jesus took his place on the cross and died for his sins.

Ivan was in shock. He could not believe that someone would love him that much. Ivan understood sacrificial love in part because of his loyalty to the gang. He knew what it meant to be willing to die for something he believed in. What blew him away was the fact that someone actually did it. Someone actually followed through, and His name was Jesus.

Ivan was so moved by God's sacrificial love that he surrendered his life on the spot. He served out the remainder of his sentence as a believer, and today is a pastor in Monterey, Mexico. It's all because someone had the boldness to share the gospel in a way he could relate to.

Ivan's story was and still is an inspiration to me and makes me want to go out and share God with the many who still need to hear the good news of the salvation through Jesus Christ. His testimony brings to mind these verses from Ephesians 2:

> It wasn't so long ago that you were mired in that old stagnant life of sin. You let the world, which doesn't know the first thing about living, tell you how to live. You filled your lungs with polluted unbelief, and then exhaled disobedience. We all did it, all of us doing what we felt like doing, when we felt like doing it, all of us in the same boat. It's a wonder God didn't lose his temper and do away with the whole lot of us. Instead, immense in mercy and with an incredible love, he embraced us. He took our sin-dead

lives and made us alive in Christ. He did all this on his own, with no help from us! Then he picked us up and set us down in highest heaven in company with Jesus, our Messiah. (verses 1–6 MSG)

When it came to the opportunities God gave me to share my music, I would always share something from the Bible beforehand. I know the only lasting change that can take place in a person must come from the Word of God and not human words, so I always try to incorporate God's Word whenever possible in my music and in the messages I share.

I am amazed at all the doors of opportunity that God has opened for me to minister to people. I have been all over California, in some of the craziest and scariest neighborhoods you can think of, to reach out and share my music and the message of forgiveness. I have been to hundreds of churches and youth events over the years since my release from prison. I have been to prison yards, county jails, and youth detention centers. I have been to juvenile halls, group homes, rehabs, and high schools. I have been to other states and other countries to share my music and His message of hope. I have even been to Durango, Mexico, hometown of the infamous drug lord, El Chapo.

I am sharing all this not so you can say, "Wow, look at all Gabriel has done." I am sharing all this so you can see all that God can do with someone who is simply willing to say yes when God calls them to do something or go somewhere for Him. Remember the words of Isaiah:

> "Also, I heard the voice of the Lord, saying:
> 'Whom shall I send,
> And who will go for Us?'
> Then I said, 'Here am I! Send me.'"
> (Isaiah 6:8)

As much as I have loved going to all these places and serving in all these areas, Santa Ana, California, has always been where I call home. I actually never imagined that God would call me back to the place that caused me so much pain and heartache and to a city where I was on my way to becoming just another statistic. But that is exactly what God decided to do. Who says that God doesn't have a sense of humor?

Slowly God was bringing opportunities to partner with local churches in Santa Ana, and whenever God opened a door for me to serve, I would walk through it. Every time I would minister to the various people in Santa Ana whom God had placed in front of me, I felt a deep connection with the people. I knew their struggles firsthand. I knew the community attitudes firsthand. I knew the gang element firsthand. And I knew what God could do firsthand to help them overcome those struggles, attitudes, and evil elements.

God gave me a heart for the city of Santa Ana, and I began to share with Tommy the desire I had to constantly minister in this city. To my surprise he shared with me the same desire and compassion for this city. So we began to host our own outreaches into the community and we would hit them with a one-two punch. I would rap and he would preach. And by God's grace, we were having some success. The more we made ourselves available, the more opportunities came our way.

Then in 2014, God led us into something much bigger than we could have ever planned or imagined. God called us to step out in faith and plant a church. As we were deciding what to call the church, God spoke directly to Tommy's heart and gave him the word *hope*. The name of the church became Hope Alive, which is the message God has given to us to proclaim. Our hope is alive because Jesus lives.

After a few years, something else amazing happened. The words that Mama Jerry had prophesied over me eleven years earlier were fulfilled. On December 8, 2016, I was ordained as one of the pastors at Hope Alive. Truly God can do "exceedingly above all that we ask or think" (Ephesians 3:20).

Today, Hope Alive also oversees a ministry called Release Time Christian Education, which is an outreach ministry to the city of Santa Ana's elementary schools. We are currently in over fifteen schools and get to share the love of Jesus with more than 450 kids every week. We also go into five different high schools in Santa Ana, where we have Bible clubs each week. God continues to show us an abundance of favor in our community.

During one of our high school Bible club meetings there was a guest listening as Tommy and I shared with the students. She was a law student at the University of Southern California, and when we were finished she gave us her card and said, "Hey, if you guys want to clean up your records give me a call. I can help you with that."

I followed up with her, and a few months later I was standing before a judge, hoping to be granted a Certificate of Rehabilitation and have my criminal record expunged for good. If all went well, it meant that my full rights as a law abiding citizen would be restored to me.

I was asked to put together a portfolio with reference letters and certificates of accomplishments I had received since my release from prison. I did just that and decided to go one step further.

There was one person I wanted to come to court with me in person. I wanted Myron, the man I shot so many years ago, to stand with me before the judge. And I couldn't have imagined the impact our reconciliation would have that morning.

Standing before the judge with my family, pastor, and friends, my attorney began to review the reasons I should be granted this petition. Then she added, "And Your Honor, Myron May is here today in court to support Mr. Nieves."

The judge immediately stopped her and asked if Myron was in court.

He stood up and said, "Yes, Your Honor, I am here."

"Please come to the stand. I want to hear it from your mouth," she said. "Please tell us all what happened and what is your side of the story."

Myron began, "Well, Your Honor, all I can say is we were all a bunch of adolescent kids with no direction. And Your Honor, I want you to know that I did not have to be here this morning, but I chose to be here. I am here because I truly believe in the change that God has done in my brother Gabriel's life."

I could see the astonishment on the judge's face. As I recall it, her statement went something like this:

> "Well, this is what reconciliation is truly supposed to look like. This morning, Mr. Nieves, when I reviewed your file, I had zero intention in granting your Certificate of Rehabilitation. But because of your story and Myron's testimony today, I am going to grant it! Congratulations, sir. Keep doing what you're doing. The State of California hereby grants you your Certificate of Rehabilitation!"

The entire court room, which was filled with people, began to applaud. Sometimes the grace of God is simply unexplainable. I love these words from Micah:

> Where is another God like you, who pardons the guilt of the remnant, overlooking the sins of his special people? You will not stay angry with your people forever, because you delight in showing unfailing love. Once again you will have compassion on us. You will trample our sins under your feet and throw them into the depths of the ocean! (7:18–19)

The last time I was in a courtroom, I was facing a life sentence. This time my family, friends, and even strangers were celebrating a changed life. Once again God had showed himself strong and gracious on my behalf.

BEYOND THE GANG

CHAPTER 8

TACKLING TEMPTATION

No temptation has overtaken you except such as is common to man; but God is faithful, who will not allow you to be tempted beyond what you are able, but with the temptation will also make the way of escape, that you may be able to bear it.
(1 Corinthians 10:13)

I was an addict. During that time of my life, I only cared about one thing: getting high. When I wasn't high, my main thought was planning when and where I was going to score drugs and get high again. My addiction was all-consuming. Addiction, however, isn't limited to the drug addict or the alcoholic; addictions come in all shapes and sizes, and each one carries its own set of burdens, struggles, shame, and guilt.

I won't pretend it has been an easy road getting to where I am today or that I haven't been tempted at times to call up my old friends and hang out. One thing I believe that has helped me keep moving in the right direction is that I have made myself accountable to other faith-filled people. I have taken the time to surround myself with people who share the same passion for God that I do, people who place the same priority on living out their faith as I do. And it has made all the difference in the world.

You do not have to be defined by your addiction. You do not have to live under its condemnation and guilt. You do not have to live defeated by its control. There is hope and help in God.

I know the struggle is real. I also know that you may have tried to kick this habit (whatever it may be) and have failed time and time again. And even though I know there is victory to be found in Jesus over every type of addiction, I also know that for some it will remain a daily struggle.

For some, God may graciously and miraculously remove their addiction as they come to Him, confess it to Him, and seek His forgiveness and healing from it. For others, He may not remove it that way but rather will call you to a life of overcoming day by day, living and resting in His grace much like God called Paul to do with his burden.

Paul asked to be free from some unknown weakness, praying to God time and time again. God responded, "My grace is sufficient for you, for My strength is made perfect in weakness." (2 Corinthians 12:9)

It was not the answer Paul wanted, but it was the decision God made. Sometimes we will be healed of our addictions when we ask God, and sometimes He will want us to walk through them learning and growing in the power of His grace.

This doesn't mean there is no overcoming sin or addiction if God doesn't remove it. It simply means it will be something for which we need to depend on Him daily. And that may be the reason He doesn't provide immediate deliverance to all who ask. As humans we are prone to wander away from God, but when we are dependent on Him we tend to stay closer, turn to Him more frequently, and trust in Him more completely. We need to exchange our self-reliance for God-reliance. For some, learning how to live in the sufficiency of God's grace is the only way they will get there.

Temptation is real, and for those facing addiction, temptation can feel crippling. We can find victory through God's Word. You may be addicted to drugs, alcohol, pornography, gambling, lust, food, money, power, or something else, but there is help in overcoming whatever addiction you might have.

First, know that being tempted is not a sin. It is when we give in to that sin with our thoughts or actions that the sin becomes a reality (see Matthew 5:27–28). Prevention is where the battle is won or lost.

Next, ask. Begin by asking God for forgiveness and help to change. True forgiveness and lasting change cannot happen apart from God. Know that God wants to help. He wants to be your strength and source of healing. Like the prodigal son, however, we must eventually see our need and then decide to change our situation and circumstances. God will be there to meet you.

Also, dig deep. Dig deep into God's Word and seek intimate fellowship with Him. The only way to become the person that God wants you to be is to spend time in His Word and in prayer. Read the Bible every day. Use other tools like devotionals, Christian books, podcasts, Christian music, and Christian radio. Use all the resources available to you, because the reality is that you are in a battle. You need every tool you can get your hands on. Consistent quality time with God is going to be the key in any victory over addiction.

Play defense. As the saying goes, the best offense is a good defense. Victory over addiction will be most effective if you stop the behavior before it even begins. Practically remove and avoid tempting influences. Fighting your sinful habits means not leaving room for those harmful desires and removing those sources of temptation. That might mean staying away from certain people, not going to certain places, using certain filters on your computer, emptying your house of certain items like alcohol and outdated prescriptions. An ounce of prevention is worth a pound of cure.

Recognize the importance of teamwork. The reality is that we need other people. One of the many reasons God established His church was so that we do not have to go through life alone. We can find help and support in the community of God. Begin by talking to someone about your struggle and seek the help and support of others. This may mean finding someone in your church that you can confide in, or it may mean going to a Christian support group. It may mean finding an accountability partner, someone you can call any time of the day or night who will be there to talk to you, no matter what, someone who even will get in the car and go meet you if that is what you need in the moment.

There is no quick fix. This isn't cake mix theology where you just add water, bake, and voilà, you have a cake! No, it is hard work.

It likely will be filled with highs and lows, tears and fears, successes and failures, and times when you feel as though you will never get through this. It likely will be filled with times when you question your love for God because of your repeated failures, times when you question your salvation, times when you feel like quitting, and times when you are on the highest mountain of great joy and happiness.

Through the mountains and valleys of overcoming addiction, remember this: "If we confess our sins, He is faithful and just to forgive us our sins and to cleanse us from all unrighteousness" (1 John 1:9).

Before you pass judgment on gang members or other members of the criminal underworld, know that according to God's law, we are all criminals. We have all broken the law, and there is a price to be paid for what we have done.

The Ten Commandments confront us with the truth that we are all lawbreakers who deserve God's punishment for breaking His law. As the Bible says: "God's law was given so that all people could see how sinful they were. But as people sinned more and more, God's wonderful grace became more abundant. (Romans 5:20 NLT).

If you are tempted to think, "I am a good person," then know that according to God,

> "There is none righteous, no, not one;
> There is none who understands;
> There is none who seeks after God. . . .
> There is none who does good, no, not one."
> (Romans 3:10–12)

To further illustrate, consider the following. Have you ever told a lie? It doesn't have to be a *big* one, like the spider web of lies associated with a calculated cover-up like an affair. No, it can be one of those so-called little white lies that you tell someone in order to spare their feelings, like "Yes, I loved it" when you didn't. Or, one of those evasive little lies you said to avoid conflict, like "Yes, I did" when you didn't, or "I forgot" when you didn't , or "It wasn't me" when it was.

Have you ever stolen anything? Again, it doesn't have to be a premeditated, highly planned bank robbery. It can be as small as taking a pack of gum as a kid or walking off with some office supplies from your employer or pocketing money that is not yours. We can try to justify our theft by thinking, "They owe me that" or "After all I have done for them, this is least they can do for me."

Have you ever thought about killing someone, or have you ever committed adultery? "Oh wait a minute," you're thinking, "now you're going too far. I would never do something like that."

Remember, Jesus taught that if we hate, it is the same as murder, and if we lust, it is the same as adultery.

The point is that God's standards are high. And the reality is that we have all broken God's law, and God requires that a penalty be paid. Jesus paid that penalty for you and me.

Jesus was not just a man, but the Son of God, born of a virgin. And because Jesus was conceived by the Holy Spirit, He was born sinless. Why is that important? It's because God only would accept a perfect, sinless, sacrifice for sin. God is holy and must punish sin. Because Christ shed His blood in our place, God the Father not only forgives our sin but also declares us righteous.

In John 3, the Bible presents an incredible picture of God's love for all people:

> This is how much God loved the world:
> He gave his Son, his one and only Son.
> And this is why: so that no one need be

destroyed; by believing in him, anyone can have a whole and lasting life. God didn't go to all the trouble of sending his Son merely to point an accusing finger, telling the world how bad it was. He came to help, to put the world right again. Anyone who trusts in him is acquitted; anyone who refuses to trust him has long since been under the death sentence without knowing it. And why? Because of that person's failure to believe in the one-of-a-kind Son of God when introduced to him. (John 3:16–18 MSG)

Because of the sin of Adam and Eve, all people will die eternally. But in Christ Jesus we are made alive. This life comes to us because God "so loved the world" (John 3:16 NKJV). Jesus Christ was born on earth, was crucified for our sins, and was raised to life by the power of God. In so doing, Jesus conquered sin, death, and the grave. When we confess that Jesus is Lord and believe in our hearts that God raised Him from the dead, we will be saved!

Salvation is not a religion. It's not rules or regulations or rituals. Salvation is a relationship, and it is a relationship that you can start today.

REAL ANSWERS TO TOUGH QUESTIONS

Why is there evil and suffering in the world?

Sometimes the question is asked in other ways: *If God is good and all-powerful, then why is there evil in the world? If God is good, then why doesn't He deal with evil?* Some wrongly conclude that since evil exists, God does not. Or, that because there is good and evil, then God must have created both, and if God made evil, then He can't be loving. Around and around we can go on this never-ending merry-go-round of faulty logic.

First, it is important to note that God is not the creator of evil. Evil is not something created; evil is the absence of good. God is, by nature, good and loving. What He does and what He creates is good, and evil results by making choices to ignore God.

Because God did not make human robots but gave us the choice to follow Him or not, the choice to live for Him or not, we have the choice to do either good or evil. When Adam and Eve disobeyed God, their choice to not do the good God had told them to do resulted in evil coming into the good world God created. God is neither evil nor created evil. Humanity brought evil upon themselves by selfishly choosing their way over God's way.

The other problem with the questioning of God's love due to the presence of evil is to acknowledge that good and evil exist. But how can we define good apart from the moral law that God has given humanity? Without God's moral law we would not even know what evil really is.

Evil is due to selfishness and self-centered choices. God allows evil, and although we do not know all the reasons He tolerates it, one thing is certain. If he wiped out evil, He would be wiping out humanity, and then no one would have an opportunity to turn to God and be saved.

How can I trust the Bible?

The Bible is unique and unlike any other book. The Bible is not only the best-selling book of all time, the most-translated book of all time, and the most-read book of all time, but the Bible is also the only God-inspired book of all time. Christianity is fundamentally and foundationally built upon the Bible, because the Bible is the Word of God, conveyed through man and intended for mankind. The

Bible comes from God and is therefore entirely error-free. God is the author.

The Bible has been proven to be historically correct. The Bible has been proven to be archaeologically accurate. The Bible also has been proven to be prophetically precise. Hundreds of prophecies recorded in the Bible already have been fulfilled, word for word, with some fulfillments coming centuries after they were written.

Jesus also trusted in and relied on the authority of God's Word. He frequently quoted it (see John 4), He repeatedly taught it (see Matthew 5), and He boldly declared its divine origin, saying, "Your [God's] word is truth" (John 17:17). The more you examine the evidence, the more you become convinced that the Bible is more than a random collection of interesting stories. The Bible is authoritative, authentic, and accurate.

If you are skeptical about the trustworthiness of the Bible, I would recommend that you do your own examination of it. Begin reading, starting in the Gospels (Matthew, Mark, Luke, and John), where you can meet the Bible's central and historical figure, Jesus of Nazareth, the One who continues to impact and change lives today, more than two thousand years later.

Where did God come from?

No one created God, because God is the only self-existent, uncaused, uncreated, eternal being. The question of where

God came from begins with a false pretext by assuming God was created. Only things that come into existence need a cause, but God never came into existence. He has always existed and always will exist. While the universe and everything in it came into existence and therefore needed a cause, God has and continues to live outside of those boundaries. Just as the creator of a computer lives outside the confines of that computer, so, too, God lives outside the confines of this universe.

Those who reject God as Creator have to believe that matter came into being without any cause. They also have to believe that life itself popped into existence without an adequate cause. This reasoning also assumes that God is limited by time, space, and matter, when in fact the One who created all of these lives outside of those constraints: "In the beginning God created the heavens and the earth" (Genesis 1:1). It may be hard to fully comprehend, because we live in, and are subject to, time, space, and matter. There is no origin *to* God—only origin *from* God.

Will you go to heaven if you are a "good person"?

There is a common perception that so long as someone leads a generally good life, they will get into heaven. The question "Don't good people go to heaven?" assumes that although some "bad" people may need punishment, most people are basically "good." As such, the notion is that good people should be allowed to enter heaven. Tied to this view is the reasoning that entrance into heaven is based our works rather than on God's grace and that in the end, as long as your good outweighs the bad in your life, you are set for eternity.

Biblically speaking, however, people are not "good" by nature. In fact, when compared to God's standards of holiness, no one is good. As Jesus said, no one is good except God alone (see Mark 10:18; Luke 18:19). Therefore, since no one is good as defined by God, then those who enter heaven do so not on the basis of their merit, but on the basis of God's grace given through Jesus Christ.

Simply put, we can't work hard enough to earn salvation. We are and never will be nice enough to gain a free pass into eternity. No one can ever claim to be good enough or to do enough good works to gain entrance into heaven. Instead, the only way to heaven is by turning to Jesus for your salvation.

Does hell really exist?

Hell is a real place. Jesus says that hell was prepared for the devil and his angels (see Matthew 25:41). People were made for God. Hell was made for the Satan. Yet people who die in their sin, without Jesus Christ as their Lord and Savior, will spend eternity in hell.

It also surprises some that Jesus had a lot to say about hell. In fact, scholars have determined that He said more about hell than about heaven. His intention was not to threaten people by the frequent mention of hell but to offer a way out of such a fate.

Definitions and descriptions of hell vary, but what we do know for certain is that hell includes being separated from God, the source of true light, love, and goodness. Hell includes torment, outer darkness, and is described as an "unquenchable fire" where there will be "weeping and gnashing of teeth" (Matthew 3:12; 8:12).

The teachings surrounding hell are key to understanding that hell's existence has less to do with punishment and more to do with the nature of God. Yes, God is loving, but He is also completely sinless, holy, and just. This means that anything unholy cannot enter His presence. As a result, those who reject His truths and choose to live apart from God also will live apart from God for eternity. Yes, God is loving, and He has made a way for all to live with Him for all eternity in heaven, not in hell. However, He does not force belief on anyone. If someone winds up in hell, it is because they have made the choice to reject God's offer of salvation.

Don't all religions lead to the same God?

There is a dizzying array of options when it comes to religion, and contemporary culture promotes that they are all equally valid. It seems absolutely bizarre to people that someone would say there is only one way to God.

God made it clear numerous times in the Old Testament that there were other gods. There were other religions, and His people were not to assume that these gods were simply manifestations of him. They were different. They were demonic. They were not of God or from God.

Any religion that does not embrace, worship, and obey Jesus as He is revealed in the Bible is a false religion. Jesus said, "I am the way, the truth, and the life. No one comes to the Father except through Me" (John 14:6). There are a number of possibilities here for why Jesus might have said this, and they can be summed up this way: Jesus was deluded or deceptive, or He was deity.

If He was deluded, then even though He might have been sincere, He was wrong in believing that He was the Son of God.

If He was deceptive, then He *knew* He wasn't God but went around telling people that He was the only way to God. In other words, He was a sinister storyteller, purposely deceiving people.

The final option is that Jesus was who He said He was and therefore was and is God. Christians did not come up with the idea that Jesus is the only way to God. That idea came from Jesus Himself. If Jesus was wrong, then Christianity is wrong. But if Jesus was right, then there is no other way to heaven apart from Him.

BEYOND THE GANG

REAL ANSWERS TO TOUGH *TEEN* QUESTIONS

Is sex before marriage wrong if both people love each other?

Although Christians would agree that "sleeping around" is wrong, some are inclined to think there is nothing wrong with having sex with the person they intend to marry, prior to actually tying the knot.

It is important to remember God is in favor of sex. He invented it after all. But God created sex with boundaries—boundaries that He set in place. This was not to be some sort of spiritual spoilsport, but to protect and enhance the experience within the marriage covenant.

The Bible says, "Honor marriage, and guard the sacredness of sexual intimacy between wife and husband. God draws a firm line against casual and illicit sex (Hebrew 13:4 MSG). And again, "God wants you to live a pure life. Keep yourselves from sexual promiscuity (1 Thessalonians 4:3 MSG).

Ultimately God's purpose and plans for sex are for our good. Because He has designed us in a particular way, He also has designed sex to be enjoyed in a particular way, which is part of His intended greater gift: that of a committed and loving relationship in marriage.

Does God hate homosexuals?

The awful reality is that some individuals who call themselves Christians have acted hatefully toward homosexuals and also promoted hateful speech against them. We need to begin by rejecting that reaction and refusing to support or condone any such sentiment or action. When it comes to homosexuality, the Bible is not outdated or out of touch with the reality and the practice of homosexuality, because homosexuality was widely practiced in different civilizations even before the time of Moses.

The Bible teaches that all human beings are created in the image of God and that human life is therefore precious. The individual has significance and dignity just by being human, and every human is loved by God. The homosexual and the heterosexual alike are both equally loved by God.

What God does hate is sin. And that is something both the homosexual and the heterosexual also share. Just like premarital sex between heterosexuals is sin, so is homosexuality.

Because God loves people, or to put it another way, because God loves the sinner and not the sin, He has made a way for both the heterosexual sinner and the homosexual sinner to be saved. For both, it requires turning from their sins and turning to God.

God can cleanse and purify any person from any sin. He is able to give deliverance to anyone who sincerely desires true freedom. Jesus died on the cross and was raised from the dead so that all might enjoy salvation and a relationship with God.

Is it wrong to smoke marijuana even when it is legal?

Even though marijuana is not mentioned in the Scriptures, we do have some God-given principles to guide and direct our thinking about this issue. Sometimes the best place to start with a question like this (and many of the other questions not specifically addressed in the Bible) is to keep our eyes on the big picture. What is the purpose of the Christian life?

If our purpose as Christians is to worship God, to love Him, and to serve Him, then we should pursue those things that help us achieve that goal.

Even recreational use of marijuana distorts reality and numbs people in their ability to experience life as it truly is. No one has ever accused someone smoking weed of being more engaged or having a better grasp of reality. Add to that what the Bible says: "All things are lawful for me, but all things are not helpful. All things are lawful for me, but I will not be brought under the power of any" (1 Corinthians 6:12). This can include weed, alcohol, drugs (legal or illegal), lust—you name it. We can be brought under the influence of many different substances, but God wants to be the main influence in our lives. Anything that might interfere with that is better left alone.

Is it okay to listen to non-Christian music or see non-Christian movies?

Let's begin with the extremes. There are definitely movies and music that God does not want you to watch or listen to. For example, music with explicit lyrics are off-limits. Movies with overt sexual content or senseless gratuitous violence are off-limits.

On the flip side, there are definitely movies and music God would support and approve of your enjoying, like praise and worship music that sings about God and our relationship with Him. Go ahead and enjoy it with a clear conscience. You can also enjoy movies that have a redeeming message or support biblical Christian values.

There may be some debate in the area of general (or secular) movies and music that, although they may not directly proclaim a Christian message, have nothing inherently wrong with them. They don't promote sinful behavior, use vulgar language, and so on.

The question then becomes how the things you are watching affect your heart, your thoughts, and your behavior. If what you watch makes you think or do things that do not honor God, then you should avoid those influences. If they are so-called harmless forms of entertainment, then each person has to determine for himself or herself which movies, music, television programs, video games, and other forms of entertainment they should allow in their minds as well as which ones they should avoid.

How can I know what God wants me to do with my life?

Discovering your purpose in life can be an intimidating prospect, but with a few simple tips, you can be on your way to discovering your purpose and God's will for your life.

First and foremost, our purpose in life begins by entering into a relationship with God. We will never be fulfilled in this life if we live apart from God.

Next, our purpose involves obeying what God tells us to do in the Bible. God often reminds us that our love for Him is demonstrated by our obedience to follow His commands, so doing what the Bible says is very important in living out your purpose in life.

Then, finding out what your talents and abilities are will go a long way in narrowing your focus with regard to discovering your specific purpose. God has given every believer a spiritual gift, so learning about spiritual gifts from the Bible will help here. The spiritual gifts are discussed in three separate passages in the New Testament: Romans 12; 1 Corinthians 12–14; and Ephesians 4. Prayerfully read these passages and see what God reveals to you about these gifts. Also, listen to others. Turn to those trusted and close friends who can share what gifts they see in you. Next, be prayerful. God has called you, and He is completely able to reveal your purpose and gifts to you. And He will as you diligently seek Him (see Hebrews 11:6).

Remember that your purpose is not just about you; it's about what God wants to do in you and through you. He has called you to a purpose and wants you to walk in it to benefit others and for your own joy. (For more on this subject read "Discovering God's Will for Your Life: Your Journey with God, by Mike Lutz)

How can I forgive someone who has hurt me?

Forgiveness is a process that begins by making the decision to forgive because we have been forgiven. Forgiveness is part of God's nature, and it needs to be part of ours as well. There is no pill we can take, and there is no express lane for forgiveness. It takes time, and it takes effort.

Begin by asking God for help. Part of that help comes by digging into the Bible and growing in your understanding of God forgiveness.

Pray. Pray for your heart to be changed toward the person who offended you, and pray that God would work in the heart of the other person.

Lastly, think positive. Don't dwell on the past, and don't stay focused on the hurt or harm. Rather, replace those thoughts with the following:

> Fix your thoughts on what is true, and honorable, and right. Think about things that are pure and lovely, and admirable. Think about things that are excellent and worthy of praise. . . . Then the God of peace will be with you. (Philippians 4:8–9 NLT)

Do I have to obey my parents even if they are wrong?

With a question like this, we should also add those in positions of authority to the scope of our answer. Do we have to obey authorities even if they are wrong? Those in authority can include teachers, police, parents, government, bosses, and so on.

When it comes to how we respond to those in positions of authority, the general guideline should be submission. We are called to submit to all those in authority over us, whether they are parents or teachers or bosses or the police. We are to accept their position of authority and follow their instruction.

The Bible makes it clear in the book of Romans:

> Let everyone be subject to the governing authorities, for there is no authority except that which God has established. The authorities that exist have been established by God. Consequently, whoever rebels against the authority is rebelling against what God has instituted, and those who do so will bring judgment on themselves. (Romans 13:1–2 NIV)

The only exception to this rule is if the authority over you requires you to disobey Jesus or the Bible. If they do, then you can refuse to obey their instruction at that point, because as the apostle Peter reminds us, "We must obey God rather than human beings!" (Acts 5:29 NIV).

We will honor God above all other authority. His instruction, His command, is higher than any other. Therefore, the ultimate law we submit to is His.

What is sin?

A sin is any thought, word, or action that falls short of God's standards or will. God is perfect, and anything we do that falls short of His standard of perfection is sin.

God's will is like the center of at target, and when we sin or fall short of His will, we miss the mark. Everyone has missed that mark on the target, as the Bible says: "For all have sinned and fall short of the glory of God" (Romans 3:23). We are sinners by nature, and we sin daily. Because Adam and Eve sinned, human beings ever since then were born with a sin nature. Because we have inherited a sin nature from Adam and Eve, we commit individual sins daily.

This is why we need Jesus, because only Jesus can forgive us of all our sins. When we believe in Jesus, we have been freed from the penalty of sin and now have the power to resist sin. As a result, we can choose whether or not to commit personal sins, because we have the power to resist sin through the Holy Spirit who dwells within us.

Will God forgive me of . . . ?

It is natural to think that more severe crimes get more severe punishments. It is also natural to think that some sins are worse than others, both in action and consequence. Although it is true that some sins carry with them far greater earthly consequences (taking a pack of gum, for example, and taking a life have vastly different consequences), all sin is a violation of God's law, no matter the varying degrees of severity.

The good news is that God is willing and able to forgive all sin. Jesus paid the price for all sins on the cross, and no sin is too small or too large for God to forgive.

Maybe you have done some things—and maybe you have done some pretty bad things and feel bad about what you have done in the past. There is forgiveness available to all who seek it. God made a way of forgiveness, not just for some sin but for *all* of it. There is no sin that God cannot forgive. No matter what you've done, God will forgive you . . . if you will come to Him in faith.

If you want to be forgiven of your sin right now, a good place to start is with a prayer like this:

> God, I know that I have sinned against You. I know that I am deserving of being separated from You forever. I know there is nothing I can do to save myself. I need Your forgiveness. You have provided a way.

You sent Your Son, Jesus, who lived a perfect life, died on the cross for my sin, and was raised from the dead on my behalf. You have paid the price for sin so that I might be forgiven. Please forgive me, God. I believe in You. Remove my guilt and help me to begin my new life with You. Thank you for providing a way of forgiveness and for accepting me into Your family. Amen.

CONGRATULATIONS! You have just made the best decision of your life. Now what? Here are a few things that will help you successfully take the next steps in your walk with God.

First, it is important to get into the Word of God, so buy yourself a Bible. We recommend starting in the gospel of John. If you need a Bible and cannot afford one, we will provide you with information on how you can get one (see below).

Next, find a Bible-teaching church to attend. If you live in or around the Santa Ana or Costa Mesa area, consider coming to Hope Alive Church. Start by visiting the website www.HopeAliveSantaAna.com.

A great tool to help you understand the Bible and how it all fits together in a practical way is a good devotional. For this we recommend *God Every Day: 365 Life Application Devotions.* (Also available in Spanish).

If you have questions, need help, or need a Bible or resources to help you grow in your walk with Christ, contact Gabriel and Mike (see About the Authors for website information).

ABOUT THE AUTHORS

Gabriel Nieves was born and raised in Santa Ana, California. At the age of fourteen he joined a local gang and began living a lifestyle of darkness that included drugs, alcohol, and violence. He was in and out of prison for a period of seven years and was on a road that led to destruction.

On December 31, 2001, he was involved in a gang shooting and was arrested shortly thereafter. He soon realized the seriousness of his crime and found himself in the Orange County Jail fighting a life sentence. After a month of being incarcerated, he was approached by a born-again believer in Jesus Christ who shared with him the love of God through the gospel. In that jail cell he rededicated his life to Jesus.

He was incarcerated for three years, but he used that time to dive deeper into God's Word and began to grow spiritually. After several miraculous events, he was released from prison.

Gabriel now serves as an assistant pastor at Hope Alive Church in Santa Ana and has a desire to reach those who are living the lifestyle he once was a prisoner of.

To find out more about Gabriel and his music, visit www.TheMessageMusic.com.

Mike Lutz loves writing inspirational, memorable, and life-changing words. He has been a golf pro, a pastor, and is currently an executive chef. When he is not cooking or creating recipes, he can be found drinking a tall glass of ice tea while writing outside on his patio.

Mike is the author of *Discovering God's Will for Your Life: Your Journey with God*; *God Every Day: 365 Life Application Devotions*; and his first novel, *The Armageddon Initiative*.

Mike currently resides in Southern California with his wife, Colette, and beagle, Cinnamon. Learn more about Mike and read his blogs at www.mikelutz.org.